A Simple Guide to Planetary Transformation

How Your Personal Spiritual Journey Can Change the World

Gregory M. Toole

Park Point Press
Golden, Colorado

Printed in USA
Published February 2013

ISBN 978-0-91136-57-3

Dedicated to my parents
William G. Toole Jr.
and Mona Toole
whose love and faith in me
over the many years
provided the fertile ground
for this book.

Contents

Foreword   xi

Acknowledgements   xiii

Introduction   1

Chapter 1: Foundation of Spiritual Principles   5
Where Do We Begin?
Spiritual Laws
The Divine Urge to Express
The Power in Your Word
One Power, One Source, One Cause
How Do We Use It?
Spiritual Practices for Chapter 1

Chapter 2: Love: Powerful Transcendence   15
What's Love Got to Do with It?
Loving Yourself Unconditionally
Loving Others Unconditionally
Receiving Love
Spiritual Practices for Chapter 2

Chapter 3: Healing: Possibility for Peace   27
Your Place of Pain
Living from Pain
Your Place of Wholeness
Living from Wholeness
Spiritual Practices for Chapter 3

Contents

Chapter 4: Authentic Expression: **39**
Fulfilling the Promise
Who Are You?
Being All You
Your Purpose
Living Your Purpose
Spiritual Practices for Chapter 4

Chapter 5: The Journey: Growth Required   **49**
Spiritual Practices for Chapter 5

Chapter 6: Worthiness: **55**
We All Deserve to Be Happy
Accepting Your Worth
Accepting the Worth of Others
Giving Only the Best
Spiritual Practices for Chapter 6

Chapter 7: Power: Getting Our Needs Met   **63**
Recognizing Your Power
Using Your Power for Good
Accepting Others' Power
Using Power Collectively
Spiritual Practices for Chapter 7

Chapter 8: Joy: Elixir of the Soul   **69**
The Joy Within
Summoning Your Smile
Being a Joyful Presence
Spiritual Practices for Chapter 8

Contents

Chapter 9: Freedom: The Spirit Demands It 75

Attaining Personal Freedom
Removing Our Binds on Others
Confronting Fear
Living from Love
Spiritual Practices for Chapter 9

Chapter 10: Surrender: It's Bigger Than You 83

Examining the Need to Control
Letting Go, Letting Go, Letting Go
Being an Instrument of the Divine
The Surrendered Life
Spiritual Practices for Chapter 10

Chapter 11: Caring: 93
You Have Done It unto Me

Honoring All Life
Letting Go of Judgment
Cultivating Empathy and Compassion
Sacred Service to Life
Spiritual Practices for Chapter 11

Chapter 12: Oneness: 103
The Antidote to Separation

Seeing God in Everything
Knowing Only God
Embodying Christ Consciousness
Spiritual Practices for Chapter 12

Conclusion   113

About the Author   117

Foreword

The book you hold in your hands is a powerful
companion to your spiritual growth. As you read
this book, be prepared to welcome a friend into
your heart. Gregory M. Toole addresses many of the
most familiar experiences we have in this modern
time—experiences of our own limitations, fears, and
doubts. He has lived them himself and offers candid
illustrations from his own life to teach us that limiting
life experiences do not have to be our life experiences.

As the pages turn to each new chapter, you will
find yourself compelled to read on. It is essential in
our personal journey to examine what we believe.
Gregory takes us into our life journey by asking us to
consider what it is to love ourselves, act authentically,
live "on purpose," express joy, care for all of life,
conquer our fears, and surrender to a greater
expression of life.

Like all good teachers who still are also students,
Gregory provides spiritual practices at the end of each
chapter. These practices allow us to deepen our journey
into the ideas and principles set forth in the chapter,
making the teachings come alive in our own life. The
information provided is inspiring, thought-provoking,
and relevant, and the spiritual practices allow us to be
engaged in our own growth and evolution.

Foreword

"There is nowhere to go, except to grow," Gregory tells us. This beautiful work of heart goes directly into

the most powerful and prominent areas of spiritual growth among us today. As we open our mind and heart to the teachings offered here, transformation happens. What better time than the present to choose to grow?

Many blessings on your journey. I know that it is supported by the conversation you are having with your divinity, facilitated by this book.

Rev. Mary Jo Honiotes
Senior Minister and Spiritual Director
Center for Spiritual Living, Denver

Acknowledgments

I am deeply grateful to the many people without whom this book would not be possible. Thank you to Rev. Dr. Elouise Oliver who introduced me to the New Thought spiritual principles on which this book is based and who was my direct spiritual teacher and role model for nine years of my most formative spiritual development. Thank you to Dr. Michael Beckwith who was my inspiration for entering into the deep mystery of sacred service to humanity. Thank you to Dr. Ernest Holmes whose writings on the Science of Mind philosophy profoundly impacted my life. Thank you to Dr. Judy Morley who edited this book with such care and an eye for detail. Thank you to David Goldberg, my publisher, who accepted this project with such love and support. Thank you to the many people who have shown me love and have influenced me in ways that shape who I am. I am deeply grateful for the love of Cynthia Cody over this past year and how she has seen deeply into my soul to mirror back to me who I am.

Introduction

I set out to write this book as a guide to those of us who really yearn for great change in our world, who want to make a difference, and yet who aren't quite sure how to do it. The truth is, we are powerful beyond measure. We are so connected with all of our fellow beings that making change in the world is actually quite simple. We begin right at home with ourselves. As Mohandas Gandhi is often quoted as saying, "Be the change you wish to see in the world."

This book takes you through all the areas of your life that may need healing and opening in order for the world to experience a renaissance in consciousness, a new way of being and expressing. Change can happen only when individuals like you and me make the shift. It will not happen by some decree of government, nor will it happen by a call to action from a dynamic spiritual leader. It will happen when, and because, each of us, one-by-one, embarks on a journey of healing, awakening, and renewal. It will happen when, and because, each of us lets go of ideas and beliefs that no longer serve us or our world. I am not speaking just of what we proclaim to believe, but more importantly of what we actually believe on a deeper, subconscious level that gets lived out every day.

The conditions of our world today do not exist because so many people want war, or because so many want to destroy the environment, or because people believe poverty is a good thing. Certainly, if we took a survey, few, if any, would indicate they are in favor of such things. And yet our world continues to experience war, the destruction of our natural environment, and poverty.

No, it is not because of our collective conscious beliefs that we experience these phenomena. It is because of deep-rooted ways of thinking and ways of being that we have not been able to transcend, and most often are not even aware that we have. Many tend to think that other people out there in the world somewhere are causing the problems. But this is mostly false. Yes, we may find people committing more heinous acts than we are. If we truly take an honest look in the mirror, however, we can see that we too are committing very similar acts on a smaller scale. The impact of our acts is less obvious, and therefore we may feel superior.

For example, we tell little, seemingly inconsequential lies, but we get upset when we find out a politician has lied to us. We act in a violent manner with our friends or family members by yelling at them, calling them names, just ignoring them, or withholding love. But we are outraged when we hear of violence that causes physical harm or rises to the level of being a crime.

I am speaking here of our collective responsibility as humanity for the uplifting of the planet. I am speaking of how each of us can make a small contribution to changing our world. The truth is, we are all one and our destinies are intertwined. The places where we blame others and point fingers are our denial of our own responsibility for creating a better world.

This book is not about our shadow—it is about our light. It is about awakening ourselves in such a way that we contribute to the awakening of humanity. It is about getting us to realize that it is not the world that is being called to wake up—it is we, ourselves, who are being called to awaken. We and the world are one and the same—awakening ourselves is awakening the world. But the world never does anything. It is each of us as individuals that do things and become something.

This book calls on each one of us to awaken. It calls on us to heal those places that represent our triggers, which put us into reaction rather than conscious response. It is about healing our need to separate ourselves from others, and it calls us instead to respond with love. Our true nature is love. That is who we are. So in our true nature we would always respond from love. When we have healed the areas of our being that are cut off from our true nature of love, we are in a place to respond always with love. When we respond always with love, we stop contributing to the madness in our world, and we start contributing to the healing of the planet.

At the end of each chapter you will find daily spiritual practices designed to complement the chapter you have just read so that you may take action within yourself with regard to the area of your spiritual life discussed in the chapter. You are encouraged to engage with these practices in earnest with all of your being. This is your contribution to freeing the planet to experience more love, peace, harmony, freedom, and abundance. Remember, it begins with you and with me. The work is within us, and not out there somewhere.

Most of all, remember the joy of being. Remember that it's about the journey and not about a destination. Moment by moment we can be the way we want the world to be, and moment by moment we shall create such a glorious world as this.

Chapter 1:
Foundation of
Spiritual Principles

Following a conscious spiritual path can be one of
the most exciting things one undertakes in life. It
involves risk, excitement, setbacks, and amazing
breakthroughs. It takes us to the depths of our being
and also to the heights of our yearning. It is a path
that is filled with amazing possibility for our lives,
and sometimes with the pain of facing some aspect
of ourselves that we previously denied. Why do we
undertake such a journey? Because at some point
the inner "yes" of our highest self's yearning to be
expressed exceeds the "no" of our deepest fears.
That which beckons us onward and forward becomes
stronger than that which would hold us in a smaller

sense of who we are. In other words, the spirit yearns to be expressed and ultimately won't be denied its opportunity. Who we truly are, in our entire splendor, seeks expression.

Where Do We Begin?

If you are reading this book, the journey has already begun. Something in you is ready—your awareness has brought you to this book. We begin with the awareness that there is more. There is more to me than just this human existence—making a living, eating, sleeping, having sex, and eventually dying. The journey begins when mere subsistence is no longer enough; when materialism no longer holds enough meaning for our lives, we seek some other reason for continuing. A voice within says, "There is more than this." Then we begin to ask the existential questions: Who am I? Why am I here? What does it all mean, anyway?

These questions have no easy or pat answers, and yet asking them opens the doorway to profound insights previously unavailable.

Therefore we must begin to dedicate some of our time and energy toward contemplation of these questions. There is a need for stillness, for just being, to begin to balance doing with being. We are called upon to be receptive as well as directive, meaning that we allow time for quiet to listen, to hear what our inner wisdom might reveal. We live with these questions and the others that naturally arise, following wherever this journey might take us.

Spiritual Laws

For some, the idea of spiritual laws could conjure up thoughts of biblical rules of conduct. Here in the context of this book, they refer to the framework and the order of our relationship to the spiritual universe of which we are a part. We are all familiar with physical laws such as that of gravity or electricity. With these physical laws we know that there are principles involved. We know that the law of gravity draws us, and everything, toward the earth, and that it is not personal in that it works the same for every person or thing.

There are also spiritual laws that respond to each person in the same way, so that they too are impersonal. They affect the outcomes in our lives. The most basic spiritual law is one of cause and effect. This law functions essentially as a clearinghouse or creative medium for our thoughts, feelings, beliefs, and attitudes. As we are to life, life will be to us. The energy of our intentions and our attention begins to create experiences in our lives and outcomes that closely resemble what is behind them, which is the real cause.

In essence, we are cocreators of our lives with the Divine. We are not passive neutral beings when it comes to our experience in life. We are not just tossed about by the wind and the sea of life and left to deal with whatever comes our way. We are active participants in creating our experience—not only by our actions, but also by some inner qualities of being that ultimately take form and physical manifestation.

The Divine Urge to Express

There is something in you that wants to express. We might say it is life's longing to be expressed in your own unique way. The very differences and uniqueness that we often try to hide in order to conform, to fit in, are the very uniqueness that is the purpose of our life, our purpose for being here on the planet. How much more beautiful and delightful would our world be if every being were expressing authentically and fully who he or she is?

The Power in Your Word

Your word, expressed as your intentions, the way you look at yourself and at life, is creative. You are a cocreator with the Divine, with life itself. Life responds to you. We are not passive beings, subject to which way the wind blows us. Most of us know this to an extent. We know that we need to make an effort, to be confident, and to take steps. Some of us even know that our word is creative and powerful. But to what extent do we believe that we create our own experiences?

First, let's distinguish between *control* and *dominion* and clear up some common misunderstandings. *Control* suggests that we direct everything—who, what, when, where, and how our life unfolds. *Dominion* is different. It suggests that we set the direction, tone, and general quality of our lives. Are we prosperous, fulfilled, and joyful? Do we have friends and meaningful relationships? In essence, is our life unfolding toward the actualization of our gifts, talents, and the most meaningful expression of who we are? Or is life about drudgery, struggle, and strain, where we eke out a living and cope with life the best we can? With dominion there is much mystery, and life is an adventure, but it's not the adventure of fear about what's around the next corner. It is the adventure of excitement in knowing it is going to be good—having joyous expectancy of how this beautiful, divine, creative essence that is within us is going to bring about, through us, this beautiful expression.

Recognizing the power in our word, we are able to have dominion over our lives. We can begin to speak and think and act in ways that reflect what we wish to experience in life. If we wish to experience more abundance, then we need to stop aligning our thinking and our words with discussions about lack and limitation, and begin shifting our conversation to be about possibility and potential. Gradually, moment by moment, as our conversation changes, both in our minds and what we verbalize, our experience begins to shift.

One Power, One Source, One Cause

One of my greatest discoveries on the spiritual path is that there is no "boogeyman." Although I certainly did not previously believe in a literal boogeyman, I did believe in a power other than good that was surely poised to mess things up at any moment, especially if things were going really well. It was as if I believed something negative or harmful was always lurking around the next corner, so I'd better be on my guard.

The realization that life is not divided against itself was very liberating indeed. The notion that life is good at its core set me free. The realization that it is I, not life itself, who works against myself at times, opened me to experience divine love. Could it be that life, the universe itself, actually loves me? If I see that the life that moves through me and through all of creation is divine, then it is not a stretch to see that as God loves me, life loves me.

Many have come to define the human ego, or the structures of our humanity that hinder us, with some sort of evil entity to be extinguished or wrestled. But the ego is not an opposing power in life. The human ego that allows us initially to adjust to being in human form also sees itself as permanent. It is not some evil power; it is simply a structure designed for our survival that needs to be transcended once we move beyond our survival need.

There is nothing to fight "out there." There is only the letting go within our own minds, within our own being, of those ideas that no longer support our highest unfolding. It is an awakening to who we truly are that is needed.

When we realize who we truly are, we can then open more fully to allow this splendor to be more fully expressed. We can let go of what have been called "morbid thoughts." Love is our essence. Love will heal us. Love will free us. And love will heal our planet. There is nothing to fight, only love to be freed.

How Do We Use It?

Imagine or remember a time when you felt as one with life and the cosmos, and when you were at ease and at peace. You were in the flow of life. All was in harmony. You were attuned with life, with the essence of who you are and with the essence of all that is. From this place you cleared away that which hindered the full expression of life through you.

When life is freed to express, it expresses joy, love, peace, abundance, and beauty.

The elements in our life that seem to hinder us, block us, or slow us down are not something to resist, fight, or fret over. They are not separate and apart from our good. Rather they are integral to our experiencing our good. They are these hurts, fears, and emotional wounds that rise to the surface so that the light of our awareness may eventually dissolve them.

This is partly what is meant by the Christian scripture in Matthew 6:33: "Seek ye first the kingdom of God, and all things shall be added unto you." The things we want to experience in life—to be, to do, and to have—are integrated with the ways that we are being called to grow spiritually. So these seeming obstacles are not problems to be solved; they are opportunities to be embraced. For example, if a person wants to become physically fit and a delivery truck shows up at his front door with a set of weights, a treadmill, and other fitness apparatus, this person has been provided the very equipment to accomplish the goal of physical fitness. Similarly, our intentions for good in our lives are matched with the very experiences we need to grow into having, being, and doing what we want.

Everything in your life is set up perfectly for you to be, to do, and to have exactly what expresses your soul, your unique essence, in the greatest way. Not a single aspect of your life is out of place or accidental. Every bit of it is there to serve a purpose for you. It has been lovingly provided to you. What will you do with it?

Our great opportunity is to grow in the ways that our soul is calling us to grow. This will result in us living exactly the life we desire to live. All of life is served when you do this. Your happiness and fulfillment are essential to the universe. Let go of the idea that this is selfish, and realize it is selfish only when you do it for purely selfish reasons. Honoring yourself is not selfish. Honoring life is not selfish.

The spiritual law of cause and effect is the power that will transform your world as you transform yourself. Align your thoughts, feelings, and vibration with love, joy, peace, wholeness, and abundance, and you will create the same in your experience, and ultimately in the world.

Spiritual Practices for Chapter 1

Affirmative Prayer:
There is only one: one divine essence, presence, and power. That one is Spirit, and its essence is oneness. I am one with the One. My nature and essence is oneness. I release any sense of smallness, unworthiness, or being less than. I embrace the fullness of my divinity. I am a perfect child of the most high. I am an inlet and an outlet for the Divine itself to find unique expression as me. I am grateful for this awareness. I give thanks for my divine nature. I let this be. All is well. And so it is. Amen.

Daily Spiritual Practice:
1. Journal about your experience of spiritual principles operating in your life.
2. List five ways your heart is calling you to express more fully.
3. List three ways that you have given power to something other than Spirit, that you are now willing to release.
4. List five higher truths you need to begin telling yourself.
5. Enter meditation for at least fifteen minutes and contemplate your life as the unfolding of your consciousness interacting with spiritual principle.

Chapter 2:
Love: Powerful Transcendence

What's Love Got to Do with It?
The answer to this question is: everything! Love is
a synonym for God. The New Testament of the
Christian Bible says, "God is love," and in some way
all religions teach some variation of this.

When we align with and attune to love we are
standing in the highest and truest sense of who we
are. There is nothing greater than love. It is what
we all want to receive, and it is ultimately what we
all want to give. We give it in our various forms. We
could say that love is why we are here, that we are
here on the planet simply to give and receive love and

to learn how to do it better, both in a human sense as well as on the soul level toward our eternal evolution.

When I was writing the first chapter of this book, after promising a chapter to my spiritual community at the end of each month, I began to fret whether what I had written was good enough. I wondered if I had made a serious mistake in promising it, and even in thinking I could write a book. I was in fear about getting it right.

Conforming to norms is one of the greatest stumbling blocks to genius that we collectively encounter. When did conformity ever produce genius?

When I turned my attention toward love, all of the anxiety and worry seemed to disappear almost immediately. In turning to love, my sole intention was to share my gifts and talents. I had no responsibility for how people would accept it or whether anyone would like it. My part was simply to give what I had to give, and allow that to be enough. I offer my love as a gift, rather than as proof that I'm okay or worthy.

In offering the gift of my writing, I felt my heart open whereas it had previously been closed by fear and worry. Opening my heart allowed the way for my gift to be expressed more fully, making my gift itself of even greater value.

What a gift it is to ourselves when we realize that we are here on this planet just to give and receive love.

The path to fulfillment is really about love. In this understanding, we are free to be fully expressed as who we are. The need to conform falls away because it is not part of our intention.

With our hearts open we may also receive love in a greater way and allow others to share their forms of expression with us. We no longer feel the need to be critical or judgmental of others; we merely accept their expression of love as the precious and unique sacred gift that it is.

Loving Yourself Unconditionally

Loving ourselves, while possibly seeming obvious, is crucial to a sane, peaceful world. So much of the violence and antisocial behavior that we experience reveals an absence of self-love at its core.

Loving ourselves is central to our overall well-being. It is so essential to healthy relationships and interactions with our environment.

To me, loving myself means valuing my unique way of expressing. It means that I am, in my essence, good and someone to be celebrated. It means it is okay to feel good about myself.

I'm not describing some narcissistic vision whereby we are self-absorbed and see ourselves as all-important. Rather, I am describing a vision of having a valid and valuable place in our world, a sense that we have something of value to contribute and share.

To go further, not only can we know this intellectually, but it can also be an embodied truth for us. That is, we actually feel good about ourselves. We feel a sense of peace, love, and joy about who we are and our place in the world.

You're probably asking, "How do we get there?" We get there by beginning to realize that our center is Spirit; therefore our center is love, and our center is goodness. Then we begin to observe all the thoughts and feelings that arise to meet and challenge this idea. They are thoughts like, "Who me?" They are false ideas that family, experiences, the world, and the media have reflected to us. More importantly, they are the unsupportive ideas about ourselves that we have internalized.

We ask ourselves, "What do I need to accept about myself? Where have I criticized and judged myself in ways that bring me down? How have I compared myself to others and thereby begun to feel less than I am?"

The answers to these questions allow us to begin loving ourselves. Our choices and decisions are powerful. In fact, it is the choices and decisions we made about ourselves in response to external events and the reactions of others that have created any self-limiting beliefs and feelings we have today. At the feeling level, a good first step is to get in touch with how we personally experience love. One approach is to bring to mind someone you find easy to love unconditionally—perhaps a baby or a pet. Then allow yourself to feel love toward that being. What does it feel like? Where do you feel it? From where does it flow? How do you expand it? How do you contract it? Essentially, get in touch with the full experience of how you love. You might do this every day for a period of two weeks.

When you feel you are fully in touch with how you experience and express love, you are equipped to begin directing that love where it is needed within your own being. That is, you are ready to begin experiencing self-love.

Now return to the idea of yourself as valuable and worthy of only good. Where in your physical body do you feel resistance to this? Allow yourself to direct love there, to that place. Allow that place to be infused and saturated with love. Continue this process for a period of days, weeks, months, or years—whatever it takes. This is a pathway to actually feeling love for yourself. Bring love into all those places where you feel unworthy, unloved, or less than whole, and into those places where you feel fear, shame, or doubt.

Love is truly powerful medicine. In reality, it is the only true cure for what ails us.

Loving Others Unconditionally
Loving others unconditionally requires that we first love ourselves unconditionally. That's what the

previous section was about.

But what does it mean to love others unconditionally? M. Scott Peck in his book, *The Road Less Traveled*, describes it as "the will to extend one's self for the purpose of nurturing another's spiritual growth." He further says, "A genuinely loving individual will often take loving and constructive action toward a person he or she consciously dislikes."

What does it take to do such a thing? Willingness. First we must see that it is valuable, and then be willing to do it. Then the ways and means have an opening through you to come forth. Before then, it is like a secret you don't have access to. But willingness is the key that unlocks that secret.

When I became a minister and spiritual teacher, I vowed that I would love all and hold animosity toward none. It is a personal vow for me that I take very seriously. It has become a spiritual practice. It is my work. Whenever I have difficulty loving someone, I recognize that I have work to do. I ask myself, what is it in this person that I have so much trouble loving? How does that quality show up in me? What place in me is touched by, set off, or triggered by this person's behavior or way of being?

Every time I am able to transcend those feelings, to get to the root of them and uproot them, I am then moved deeper in my understanding and embodiment of unconditional love. In embodying it, it becomes part of me, a part of who I am. My capacity to love has now expanded.

This spiritual practice of loving everyone and then going within whenever I find it difficult to love is one of the greatest paths to spiritual growth and further enlightenment that I have found. It doesn't leave "wiggle room." There is nowhere to go, except to grow.

Now this doesn't mean we have to spend time with every person, or that we need to stay in an unfulfilling relationship. It means only that we are to show each person love, to wish only the best for them, and generally to have thoughts and feelings of goodness toward them.

In her book, *Alchemy of the Heart*, Elizabeth Clare Prophet says, "Love is measured by the actions we take." This provides a more enlightened definition of love that goes beyond mere sentiments or words. It is about being conscious that we have choices and reflecting in our actions, choices of our highest-most intention of love.

Sometimes, or perhaps often, unconditional love that we extend to others is not returned back to us. It helps if we remind ourselves that love is the most powerful and transcending force there is. Therefore when we love, something does happen, always, even if at the most subtle and seemingly intangible level. From a purely selfish point of view, whenever we love unconditionally, we move into greater alignment with our own true nature, our own essence.

Ultimately, love is our personal salvation and the salvation of the world. Love heals all. Love is what restores us to our innate wholeness. The more love we give, the more we stand in who we truly are, and the more healing energy and light we bring into our world—individually and globally.

What a great way we can make a difference—extending love to everyone whom we meet or encounter. This is truly what the world needs more of—"love, sweet love," as the song goes.

Receiving Love
To completely be in the flow of love, in addition to loving ourselves and loving others, we let love in so that we receive love. All that we want for ourselves, materially and otherwise, are forms of love. To be completely open to receive love is to open ourselves to be fulfilled in life.

When we close ourselves off from receiving love, we narrow the avenues through which Spirit, or the universe, can bring good into our lives. Much of our good will ultimately come by way of other people—a job offer, an introduction to a life partner, a material gift, some good advice, assistance with a task, tending to the physical body.

And the trick is, we usually don't know which people

Spirit will use to bring forth our good. It could be someone with whom we already have a close relationship, but it could also be the person at the next table in a café or restaurant, or even the person in your life who, you are sure, was sent only to annoy you.

In my own life, one of the two people who introduced me to the New Thought spiritual tradition that became a central part of my life was someone who had previously been my nemesis on a professional board. At a "chance" meeting at a social gathering hosted by a mutual friend we agreed to explore what it was that caused us to view each other in such negative terms. In a fairly short time, by talking about it, we were able to see that we had each made some incorrect assumptions about the other.

Shortly after that, this person suggested I go to the spiritual center she attended, thinking it might be of interest to me. What was to follow was my discovery of a community of people on a journey similar to my own. It turned out to be one of the most important and profound turning points in my life, and it only could have come about by opening myself to receive love from a most unlikely source.

Without that experience, the book that you are reading would not exist.

In addition to the benefit we derive from receiving love, we also provide a great benefit to others by allowing them to love us. It gives others the opportunity to express, to share, and to give of their gifts and talents.

While it has been said that it is better to give than to receive, this is only partly true. It is true that giving is generally what puts us in the flow of life, what primes the pump, and what allows us to become larger by thinking beyond just ourselves. However, we are made complete only by the balance of giving and receiving. It is not that we are looking to receive when we give something, but that we are open to receive—that we recognize this as the nature of life, that there is ebb and flow. It is like breathing—in order to continue exhaling we must balance it with inhaling.

Our cultivation of love will truly be a key part of what transforms our planet. If we can learn to give and receive love ourselves, and support others in doing the same, we are contributing to healing the core thing that ails our world. Love has everything to do with it all.

Spiritual Practices for Chapter 2

Affirmative Prayer:
There is only one: one divine essence, presence, and power. That one is Spirit, and it is pure divine love. I am one with the One. My nature and essence is divine love. Right now I see and accept love as the essence of who and what I am. Divine love in this moment infuses all that I am, and that I do, and all that I have.

Past, present, and future are all one in this moment of the eternal now. Love infuses my past, my present, and my future. Every experience I have had, am now having, and will ever have is infused with divine love. Therefore, my life story is a love story. Regardless of what has happened or is happening, I now see it for what it is: the unfolding of divine love. My whole life and experience is now defined by divine love. I am transformed and made new by this realization. I open myself to experience the love that is my divine nature. I tell the story of my life as a love story, and so all in my life now conforms to the idea and reality of love. I give thanks for this awareness. I give thanks for the love that is the totality of my experience. And I simply relax into this truth. I let it be. All is well. And so it is. Amen.

Daily Spiritual Practice:
1. List one hundred things you love about yourself.
2. List one hundred things you love about life and your fellow beings.
3. List ten ideas you have had about yourself that you are now releasing because they are unlike your nature as divine love.
4. List ten ideas you have had about life or others that you are now releasing because they are unlike the nature of all as divine love.
5. Enter meditation for at least fifteen minutes and contemplate your nature as that of divine love.

Chapter 3:
Healing: Possibility for Peace

Your Place of Pain

Although thinking about our place of pain may not seem an enticing way to spend an afternoon, it is utterly important to our spiritual path and to our ultimate enjoyment of life. Until we become more conscious, so much of our expression is simply an automatic response from our place of pain. Our place of pain becomes the filter through which much of our life is lived. We respond to people and situations not from who we are, but from automatic triggers established from past pain.

So many people can be classified as the walking wounded. On the surface all appears to be okay, but beneath there is a plethora of triggers established by their unhealed past.

When I was in college, what could be considered my first true love relationship—albeit a relatively short one—ended abruptly in the middle of a semester. I found myself in the middle of the campus, sobbing uncontrollably. At the time I was one who definitely felt that "boys don't cry," and thus I felt very embarrassed after the episode. At that moment I resolved that this would never ever happen to me again. I would never again allow myself to become emotionally vulnerable.

Some fifteen years later I discovered what I had unwittingly set in motion. During those previous fifteen years I had not experienced a deep meaningful relationship to speak of. I began to ask myself why this was so. It was then that I remembered the resolution I had made to myself years earlier—that I would never again become emotionally vulnerable. Essentially, this meant I would never enter an intimate, meaningful relationship.

Many of us have similar, seemingly minor decisions, choices, attitudes, and beliefs we adopted at a key moment, usually involving much pain at some point in our past, likely as a child or young person. These are now buried deep within us, yet they guide so much of how our life currently unfolds.

This is our place of unresolved pain from the past that has us on autopilot today regarding how we respond to people and situations.

By bringing our awareness to these places of pain, by bringing them into the light of day, we can then begin to examine them and ask if they are serving us well.

Pain can take many forms, and often we have one or two dominant areas that touch almost every area of our lives. For some it is the belief that they do not matter, often stemming from childhood experiences with a parent or other authority figure. Perhaps they had several siblings and interpreted the lack of attention from parents to them at a key moment as "I don't matter. My needs aren't important."

For others it might be about being excluded, a fear they'll be left out. Perhaps this person was always the last one chosen when choosing sides in sporting matches.

For others it might be, "I am not enough." Maybe as children no matter what grade they brought home on their report card, it wasn't good enough for their parent or guardian.

The list of possibilities and examples is endless, as we all have developed beliefs about ourselves, life, and our place in life that now operate as filters for every experience we have today.

It should be noted that it is not actually what happened that causes us difficulty. It is how we interpreted what happened, and what we internalized as a result of what happened. We internalized it as a way of being that is present today just as if the event itself happened today.

Living from Pain

I call these "places of pain" because they are literally places within us where we experience hurt, pain, or fear that is powerful enough to drive our behavior. It is lodged within us and may even manifest as physical symptoms and disease.

But here I want to discuss how it manifests in our behavior, how we live our lives from these places of pain. In the case of a person who has concluded that he doesn't matter based on his early interpretation of the behavior of others, as an adult this manifests in many ways. It may manifest as experiencing one abusive relationship after another. Since the person believes he doesn't matter, the abuse may seem rather justified—"I probably deserved it," he might say consciously or unconsciously. It may also manifest as a person who is always trying to matter—one who may be described in a derogatory sense as a loudmouth. This person always needs to be heard, and no matter how much he is heard, it is never enough.

When we live from these places of pain, no amount of external stimulus is enough. There is an insatiable need. Because the underlying belief still exists, everything external simply addresses the effect and therefore is only of temporary satisfaction. The person in this last example is still left with the feeling and belief that "I don't matter." Others can assure him, "Yes, you do matter. Of course you matter. You make such a difference in my life." But somehow it doesn't soothe the deep-seated ache.

While seemingly a mystery, it is a mystery only until we become aware of what is taking place—that we have a deep-rooted belief about ourselves that needs to change.

How do we discover these deep-rooted beliefs? It begins with asking questions: Why did I react that way? Why did that incident bother me so much? Why do I never seem to be satisfied? This is not necessarily an analytic process because the answers are already within us. So there is nothing to figure out. We are asking ourselves questions that we already know the answers to but forgot, because we haven't thought about them in a long time.

The moment we ask the question, the answer begins to surface. Maybe not today, maybe not this week, but eventually, perhaps in a quiet moment, in the shower, in a dream, or during meditation, there it is—the "aha!" Yes, I have this belief that I'm not enough. Or, I always sabotage things so that I won't have to be so disappointed if they don't work out.

In meditation, we may simply ask the question and then sit in the stillness, not thinking about the question, but just being with it. When we come out of meditation we might journal about it, again asking the question and writing our thoughts and feelings about it. If an answer comes, we might ask a follow-up question. For example, you might have an insight that you don't try new things because of fear. The follow-up question might be "What is it I fear?" And let's say an answer comes—"I might fail." Then another follow-up question, "What if I do fail—what would there be to fear about that?" We continue along these lines like peeling back layers of an onion until at last we arrive at the core—the locus of power, the hidden belief in its clearest articulation. This is what drives the whole thing. Getting to this core underlying belief may happen in one sitting, or more likely over the course of many sittings.

Your Place of Wholeness

Our highest nature is one of wholeness. At our core, this is who and what we are. When we come to center, we find wholeness. We find that all is well. There is a place within us of peace, harmony, love, and joy that is not dependent upon external situations or events. This is our center.

Where do we find it? Essentially we find it everywhere within us when we align with, see, and know our true nature—that is, when we see and know ourselves as we really are.

Spirit is present at every point within us and at every point all around us. So we find our place of wholeness wherever we look for it, wherever we recognize and open to the presence of Spirit to be expressed.

How do we do this? The simplest and most straight-forward answer is through the practice of meditation, mindfulness, or some form of stillness. We pause and stop all of our doing and just allow ourselves to be. At first we may find anything but wholeness when attempting to enter the stillness. All of this doing that has dominated most of our lives has created a mind that is literally running wild.

But with practice, a little each day, maybe more with each coming day, we eventually begin to get a glimpse or a fleeting awareness of this wholeness at our center. We affirm, "Yes, wholeness is at my center." We say, "I now open myself to experience this wholeness. I now let go of confusion and drama. I recognize God is at my center. I open to sense the Presence of God, Infinite Spirit, at my center."

Because this is the truth about us, as we turn to it, we begin to know it, sense it, and experience it. Once we fully learn to come to our center, we forever have a sanctuary within us where we can bring any challenge or situation to the altar of our inner sanctuary, and there see it for what it truly is. There we may be freed from the ill effects of whatever is taking place in our lives.

Right there at our center, when we are anchored in the Presence of Spirit, there we discover that all is truly in divine order, that all is truly well. This becomes more than a platitude, more than something we've read in a book, or some intellectual idea we've accepted as true. This sense of well-being now becomes real for us; it becomes something we actually experience.

Then we have a different response when problems and challenges arise. Rather than toil and tinker, struggle and strain, or worry and fret, we see them as a call to come to center. We enter our inner sanctuary and shut the door, turning away from all conditions and turning toward a higher, more transcendent truth.

"God, or Spirit, is greater than all of this. And God can be found at my center. Let me now spend some time communing with God. Let me again remember who and what I am in the highest sense and in my eternal essence."

We remember, "I am that I AM." I am one with the Divine, with God. All that God has is mine to use. All that God is, that is my nature. I am one with all that is. No person or situation is separate from God or separate from me. There is a divine order to it all, an interconnectedness to all that is taking place in my life. I don't have to struggle against it. For it is all there for my good, for my spiritual evolution. We are then able to ask, "How is God, the Universe, using this person or situation to help me evolve spiritually?" From this place of centeredness, everything is good. Everything in our life serves a higher purpose. There is nothing to fight or battle.

Now we can simply be grateful that all is well. My life is moving forward. I am awakening to a greater sense of who I really am.

Living from Wholeness

Living from wholeness is living from our center, or in other words, being centered, being grounded in truth. The truth is that I am one with God and one with all of life, and that God's essence is wholeness. Therefore, my essence is wholeness.

When we confront a situation at work, we remember, "This is not separate from me, nor separate from God, nor separate from good." We remember where within our physical body and in what way we experience wholeness. We've been there, and we've had an experience of it already, so we know. What is it like when I go deep in meditation? Let me carry this feeling, this sense of wholeness, of well-being, into this situation before me.

Whereas our habitual human response might be to get angry, frustrated, or anxious, we remember that all is well; I have a sanctuary of wholeness, peace, and harmony right within my being. Let me go there now in my mind, in consciousness. And let me bring this situation into my inner sanctuary. I bring it into the light of truth within me, and there transform, transmute, and transcend it.

Spiritual Practices for Chapter 3

Affirmative Prayer:
There is only one: one divine essence, presence, and power. That one is Spirit, and it is pure wholeness. I am one with the One. My nature and essence is wholeness. I live from my nature of wholeness. I now release any idea of being less than enough. I am whole, perfect, and complete as a divine expression of Spirit. I open my entire being to now experience wholeness in every aspect of my life. My physical body aligns with the vibration of wholeness, and I am healed. My relationships reflect my wholeness. My relationships are healthy, balanced, and soul-nurturing for me and all others. My finances reflect my wholeness, showing forth abundance, order, and good stewardship. My work and creative expression reflect my wholeness. I am fulfilled in what I do, and it is aligned with my soul's longing to be expressed. I give thanks for my awareness of wholeness as my nature. I give thanks that my entire life is an expression of wholeness. And I simply let this be, knowing it is the truth of my being. All is well. And so it is. Amen.

Daily Spiritual Practice:
1. Remember five painful stories from your life and retell those stories from the place of your wholeness.
2. Remember five uplifting stories from your life and retell them from your place of wholeness.
3. Consider five difficult current events stories and tell them from a place of your wholeness and the wholeness of all involved.

4. Consider five positive current events stories and tell them from the place of your wholeness and the wholeness of all involved.

5. Enter meditation for at least fifteen minutes and contemplate your nature as wholeness.

Chapter 4:
Authentic Expression:
Fulfilling the Promise

Who Are You?

Anything you can say about God is true about you.
Anything you can't ascribe to God, you cannot ascribe
to be the truth about you. You are the Divine in
expression. You are what God is. Qualities like love,
wholeness, and perfection describe God, and they
also describe you.

Often we describe ourselves in terms of our
experiences, habits, roles, our career or profession,
gender, race, ethnicity, or other categories. These are
not who we are, not really who we are. These are
merely temporary experiences and ways of being that

are the outward expression of some deeper, more profound eternal essence that transcends all of these outward descriptions.

We are a unique way that Life is having expression in the world. We are a unique essence of the Ultimate.

Who we really are is able to observe all of these outward expressions. Who we are can be aware that we have a body to express with, and yet we are not our body. Who we are can observe our reactions to people, events, and circumstances, and yet, with expanded awareness we can have a degree of detachment from these reactions and say, "I am not my reactions." Who we are has choice and dominion and is capable, with expanded awareness, of responding differently to our experiences. We have the faculty to declare, "I choose something different now."

We are not better or worse than anyone else. We are not our accomplishments, and we are not our failures. We are not the things we have done, nor are we what we have not done.

You are the essence of the Divine. You are beautiful, worthy of all good. Your essence is peace, harmony, love, joy, and wholeness. You have within you the possibility of expressing great good and great harm, and yet your essence, at your core, is good. On an eternal scale you can be headed only toward good. It is who you are.

You must let go of any idea of yourself as anything but good, divine, and miraculous. Then you may begin fully living from your true essence of wholeness, harmony, and love. Your nature of light and love then may be fully expressed and you will be a beneficial presence to all with whom you come into contact.

When you accept and claim your inherent divinity and inherent goodness, then you may express your unique gifts and talents without morbidity, fear, and self-doubt. You'll realize, "I'm just here to express love, and my gifts and talents are the ways I express love." You no longer strive to earn your self-worth, to justify your existence, or to justify your worthiness to be happy.

The truth is, you are already worthy of being happy by virtue of who and what you are, not based on what you have done or will do.

With this awareness you are free to be fully expressed.

Being All You
Many of us spend a good part of our lives trying to justify our existence, or downplaying our expression so we don't offend anyone. We spend a lot of time conforming—what clothes we wear, how we act, walk, even dance, sing, or talk. Over and over we are confronted with the ultimatum—conform and you will be rewarded; stand out and you will suffer.

We are told, "Boys aren't supposed to be that way," or "Girls are supposed to be this particular way." "You're too young or too old for a particular activity or behavior."

Yet conformity prohibits you from being fully expressed, because we are not automatons or robots. We are absolutely, unequivocally unique. We are fully expressed and most fulfilled only when our uniqueness, the fullness of who we are, is honored and allowed expression.

To the extent that our behavior is not harmful to others, either physically or emotionally, the Divine is meant to be expressed through us. Of course, what is truly the divine urge cannot be harmful.

Being all you is allowing the Divine to express in the unique way that only you can express—your unique essence of Life. When you don't allow that expression, it is as if a great potential gift to the world and to Life is never realized, never given, never received, even though it had the potential to bring joy, love, light, inspiration, and healing.

Think of all those who have touched the planet and its inhabitants for years, centuries, and millennia in immeasurable ways simply because they were willing to be unique, different, and all of who they were.

Whether you are remembered after you leave this life, or have fifteen minutes of fame, is immaterial. Your gift given is meaningful and more profound than you could ever imagine.

It is as if the entire cosmos rejoices when your unique inlet and outlet of God are given. Somewhere within every being something is touched when this divine event unfolds. Even those who have never met us, those on the other side of the world, feel something even if in an ever-so-subtle way. Maybe it's so subtle as to be imperceptible, but when one is authentically expressed, we are all touched in deep and meaningful ways.

Will you dare to be all of you? The entire cosmos awaits your answer and its destiny rests in your hands, so choose wisely and lovingly.

Your Purpose

Many people are stymied by trying to find their purpose. They might say, "If I could just find my purpose, then I'd really put my energy into life." The truth is you have been fulfilling your purpose all of your life. Your purpose is to be you, to be as much of you as you can. All of your life you have been as much of yourself as you could be.

Is an oak tree ever confused about its purpose? No, an oak tree always knows it is an oak tree and spends its life being an oak tree. As humans, we must be careful here, lest we construe this to mean we are limited by our current definition of ourselves or someone else's current definition of us.

Let us be clear that you are a magnificent, unique expression of Spirit. Your purpose is to express that magnificence in the unique way that is your essence.

So because you have always been you, and you have always been expressing you, you have always been fulfilling your purpose.

As we get more in touch with our purpose, we can simply align with it in a greater and more conscious way. This is largely a process of self-acceptance, of accepting our value and our worth. Most of us have hidden for so long from being who we are that we can't possibly see any value in being ourselves.

The adage we've often been given when feeling insecure is, "Just be yourself." This is good, but actually very difficult for many people because we have been out of touch with who we are. We have become a collection of behaviors and ways of being that please others and get us rewarded socially, but to see ourselves authentically is challenging at first. Ultimately it is not very difficult at all as we connect to our hearts and remind ourselves of what we yearned for as children, what we have always secretly wanted to do, be, and have.

It's really that simple—give yourself permission to be you. Give yourself permission to be and have what is the deepest-most longing of your heart. This is actually Life's longing to be expressed uniquely as you.

We must move out of our incessant need to be approved by others, society, family, and friends. More is at stake than that. Life itself wants to be expressed uniquely as you. Who are you to deny Life's expression?

Let's pause for a moment to realize that Life's longing is about love, joy, beauty, peace, harmony, and things of our highest nature. Life's longing is never about judgment, criticism, selfishness, greed, dishonesty, or doing harm. In realizing this, we can distinguish our unique expression of Life from the lower aspects of our human existence that sometimes masquerade as who we are. These are not who we are.

When we witness people operating from the lower realms, we need not condemn, judge, or feel that they need to be punished. That is not who they are. In fact, they are acting in ways inconsistent with their own nature. Contrary to oft-stated opinions, there isn't a single person anywhere whose nature and essence are evil. There are, of course, those who have so lost their way that they identify with the lower realms and end up causing great harm and even destruction. Even then, our role is not to punish or condemn, but to wake them up, to put a mirror of truth in front of them so that they may at last see who they truly are.

Living Your Purpose

Once one realizes and accepts that it's "okay to be me," there's nothing more to figure out. It remains only to open one's heart, mind, and entire being to allowing Life to express. It's there. Can you feel it?

Can you feel Life moving in you? Now you just have to allow it to come forth. It's ultimately not hard to be what we are naturally. In fact, life is much easier once we are set free.

Now, every day and each moment ask, How would Life like to be expressed as me today? You don't need to get a concrete answer. Just ask the question and then be open. See if you can be in an attitude of openness, and trust Life. Notice when you are critical of yourself or when you are holding back. See if you can let go a little, be a bit less rigid and structured. Can you go with the flow a little more, paying more attention to the process of life unfolding, and less attention to specific outcomes and results? See if you can "trust the process," as the saying goes.

This is a way of living. Some have called it living by grace. Something quite extraordinary happens in allowing Life a unique inlet and outlet through our being. Life is infinitely wise and intelligent, whereas our human intelligence, while quite impressive, is finite. In allowing Life to move us, we are gaining access to infinity—infinite creativity, intelligence, and resources. We start to find ourselves drawn to what we need and at times having it come right to us.

More importantly, we start to feel happier, more fulfilled, and free. We begin to see life more clearly as we are freed from trying to attain and accomplish, and are content just to be expressed in the highest possible way in this moment.

Even major events, like tragedies and the personal ups and downs of others, don't seem to throw us off as we simply ask, "What can I bring forth in this situation? What's the best way I can bring my unique essence to this situation?" We are no longer trying to fix things and solve problems. We don't see problems. We see opportunities to create something new.

Can you accept that your presence makes a difference, and can you allow that to be enough? Because you are unique, you always have something unique to contribute—your "you-ness."

This is how you live your purpose—by bringing your "you-ness" to every situation. This requires taking risks because your "you-ness" will usually set you apart. You will be noticed and sometimes even criticized, but usually you will be loved and valued for your authenticity. Somewhere, deep down within each one of us, we know this is real. Yes, this is what I'd like to have the courage to do. And each time you do, you give others permission to be authentically who they are. What a tremendous gift you are to the planet.

Spiritual Practices for Chapter 4

Affirmative Prayer:
There is only one: one divine essence, presence, and power. That one is Spirit, and it is pure authenticity. I am one with the One. My nature and essence is authenticity. I live from my nature of authenticity.

I am a unique divine emanation of Spirit, meant to have unique expression in this life. As there is none other just like me, I allow myself to fully express my uniqueness as God's gift to me and as my gift to all others. My purpose is clear, and I am always on purpose. I open my heart and entire being to see clearly my purpose. I accept that being me is the highest way I may express my purpose. I release all ideas of imitation and conformity, and I allow my uniqueness to shine forth boldly. I give thanks for my uniqueness. I give thanks for my awareness of this truth, and I give thanks for my genuine individuality. I let this truth be. All is well. And so it is. Amen.

Daily Spiritual Practice:
1. List five ways you have tried in the past to conform to others' ideas of who you should be. How could you let these go?
2. List five things that make you uniquely who you are. How could you express these aspects of yourself more fully?
3. An oak tree's purpose is to be an oak tree. What is your purpose?
4. Journal about what your life would be like if you were fully living your purpose.
5. Enter meditation for at least fifteen minutes and contemplate your nature as a unique representation of Spirit.

Chapter 5:
The Journey:
Growth Required

One way or another, we are bound to grow as Life
seeks particularization through us and as us. Whether
with grace, or by stumbling every step of the way,
growth is the inevitable result. What do I mean by
growth? Growth is the revelation of the reality of our
existence. For example, if we constantly seek material
gain in order to be happy, again and again we see
that the resulting form of happiness is shallow and
fleeting. For some of us, shallow may be enough, at
least for now, but ultimately our soul's desire is for a
life of deeper meaning, something more substantial.
For some, the path will lead to cynicism—what's
it all worth anyway? For others, it will be a path of

continuously striving for things outside themselves to be happy, continuing to believe if they just have more money, a better job, a better partner or spouse, then they'll be truly happy. Each time, however, the happiness doesn't last.

As we begin to become more conscious, more aware, at some point the idea dawns upon us—maybe more of these material things will never be enough. If this is true, where do I find meaning? What will make me happy?

In my own life, I had earned a master's degree from one of the top educational institutions in the world and had a career where my salary was constantly increasing. I had respect, access to connections, a new luxury car, home ownership, friends, love relationships—all the things I had believed would make me happy. Maybe I could still have had more, but if having all of that didn't make me happy, what would make me think having more of it would? It's like eating a particular type of food, not finding it satisfying, and then trying to get more of it in hopes that more will somehow be satisfying.

This is a point of spiritual or existential crisis. Yet if we open to where this point on the path might take us, it could be an opening to a more meaningful life. It could be the greatest gift in opening the way to a dimension of life that we previously hadn't realized. We may turn inward. Perhaps if all these things outside me have not, in and of themselves, brought lasting happiness, just maybe it can be found within me. Perhaps it's so close that I've missed it. Perhaps it's so simple that my complex approach to life has overlooked it.

Someone once said to me, "I get some of these simple spiritual ideas, but what I don't understand are all the complexities of our world." Perhaps we're not here to understand the complexity, but rather to understand the utter simplicity—all of life is one. I am you, you are me, and we are one.

Some people are generally happy, and yet there is still a nagging emptiness or hollowness to the happiness, which reminds me of a story I heard of a dog that was whining and squealing. A young boy asked his father why the dog was making these noises. The father replied that the dog was sitting on a tack, to which the boy replied, "Well why doesn't he just get up off it?" The father said, "Because it doesn't hurt enough." Sometimes as humans we're not exactly fulfilled, but there's also nothing hurting enough for us to do something differently.

Here begins our opportunity for regular spiritual practice. Spiritual practice is activity and attention given at regular intervals to nurturing and communing with our inner self, our inner world.

Within us is a vast universe, infinite in its nature. What do we mean by within? This question can only truly be answered when we begin to value being, in addition to valuing doing. We live in a world where most of us are accustomed to doing, but few of us are accustomed to being. Being is about our awareness and mindfulness. It is less about what is happening than how we feel, respond, and react to what is happening. What is our personal experience of what is taking place all around us?

Spiritual practices include, for example, meditation, contemplation, reading spiritual texts, prayer, attending worship or celebration services, and other forms of activity for the purpose of expanding our awareness and experience of life. These are activities that allow us to give attention to the less tangible and more subjective inner realms of being. Is there a spiritual dimension to my being? And what does spiritual mean? Spiritual generally refers to some dimension or experience that transcends or is beyond the experience of the five physical senses. Most of us have had experiences that would fit into this category. Some have experienced a sense of oneness or connectedness to all of life in nature. For others, upon awakening they have had a moment of great clarity where they saw the meaning behind all things, even if only for a moment. And still for others it might be something more subtle, like a momentary feeling that they couldn't explain and yet sensed that it was truly meaningful in some deep way.

A spiritual practice like meditation is an opportunity to be still, to listen and be aware of the inner world. Many initially feel they are not "good" at meditation because they look upon it as another "doing" activity, something to accomplish, to conquer, to achieve, and get right. Yet meditation is not about results, but instead about process. It is not about a destination, but a journey, a path of awakening, always in process, ever unfolding. And it's not linear or sequential, nor does it occur in clearly defined steps. It simply is what it is, unique for each practitioner.

The very act of engaging in spiritual practice is a major step. The act of saying yes to spiritual practice opens the door a little further, allowing the novitiate a peek at a world previously unknown. It is an act of faith, trust, or mere openness that has its own rewards. However, it is important not to strive for this glimpse, but simply to be open to the experience.

By having a conscious spiritual practice, you expand your experience of the spiritual dimension of your being, and ultimately live a more conscious life with the possibility for greater meaning.

Spiritual Practices for Chapter 5

Affirmative Prayer:
There is only one: one divine essence, presence, and power. That one is Spirit, and its essence is of evolution. I am one with the One. My nature and essence is evolution. I let go of all resistance to my growth. I welcome change and newness. I allow Spirit more fully in my life. I live from my center in joyous expectancy of new revelation and new realization.

My life is an adventure as Spirit is always unfolding something new in my life. I am in deep gratitude for the evolution constantly taking place along my path. I give thanks for change and newness. I let this be. All is well. And so it is. Amen.

Daily Spiritual Practice:
1. Journal about where you feel stuck on the spiritual journey.
2. List five things you want to release to allow more room for Spirit in your life.
3. Journal about what is your cutting edge for spiritual growth.
4. List up to five daily spiritual practices you could commit to right now.
5. Enter meditation for at least fifteen minutes and contemplate your life as the continuous unfolding of Spirit.

Chapter 6:
Worthiness:
We All Deserve to Be Happy

Accepting Your Worth

At a Buddhist meditation retreat some years ago I heard a saying: "May all beings everywhere be happy—may all beings everywhere be well." I find this to be a beautiful sentiment that, if practiced universally, could create world peace instantly. When we want everyone to be happy and well, we put ourselves in a state of mind that recognizes the truth about our oneness. In reality, I am you and you are me.

It really comes back to accepting that we are worthy of happiness. On the surface, most of us would say that we deserve to be happy, but if we look below the surface, most of us have bought into some degree of unworthiness.

Beliefs like, "who am I to be wealthy, successful, or to have the life I really want?" indicate our sense of unworthiness. Many of us have given up on truly being happy and have settled for some form of rationalized happiness. We use rationalizations to convince ourselves we are happy.

Too many dreams and ideals are deferred or given up entirely. This is not to say that we should not let go of some of our youthful fantasies. In my youth I played a lot of sports and often fantasized about being a star athlete. Ultimately, I made conscious choices to direct my energy and attention in other directions. Whether I could have become a professional athlete or not is irrelevant, as I made choices that were the most empowering to me.

It is disempowering when there is something we want to do and we stifle it out of fear or some sense that we are either unworthy or inadequate to our desire.

Happiness does not ultimately come from doing or achieving, and yet it is hard to be happy without giving our gifts and using our unique talents. It is not the result that brings happiness, but the act of surrender to the divine urge within us. The fulfillment is in the process of acting, regardless of results.

The athlete in me still yearns to be activated, so on the weekends I play tennis and basketball. I'm not a professional, but that part of me gets attention, and in those moments I am in bliss, not necessarily because I score a point, but because I get to run, jump, pivot, spin, and exert my energy purposefully toward the ball. It is a beautiful dance, and it is enough for me in that area of life. No result is needed.

We can usually make peace with not achieving some goal. It is harder to make peace with never having tried, never having even been in the game.

Worthiness can be addressed on so many different levels: our general sense of being worthy of happiness, our sense that what we have to offer is of worth, as well as our own sense of being worthy of demonstrating a great gift or talent that we know we have. The last one could take the form of "How could I be worthy of such a great gift as this?" I remember the first mystical experiences I had, when some of the deep secrets of the universe were revealed to me. I felt a great sense of unworthiness at the time.

I have since learned that what makes me worthy is to accept and fully use the talents I have with gratitude and humbleness—not unworthiness, but humbleness. In humbleness, I recognize that all of my innate abilities are of God. I humanly did not do anything to possess them. They are simply God-given. Mine is to accept them with gratitude, recognizing that I am worthy of all that God is, as me.

Accepting your worth begins with accepting who
you are—not your human-hood, but your divinity.
When we realize our true nature, then worthiness
becomes natural. Part of understanding who we
are lies in identification. Our identification with our
human-hood has us identify with fear, pain, doubt,
failure, uncertainty, and smallness. Our identity with
our divinity has us identify with love, grace, evolution,
wisdom, intelligence, harmony, wholeness, and peace.
Our divinity is identified with infinitude. Our divine
self has never failed. From the perspective of eternity,
perfection describes our journey and our path. All
fits well in a perfect harmonization of our soul's
unfolding.

Accepting the Worth of Others
Accepting our own worthiness paves the way to
accepting the worthiness of others. When we know
our divinity, we know it for others.

When we see that each person is a unique
demonstration of the Divine, of the infinite, we see
that each person's unique abilities being utilized makes
us all whole. When we see that one person's offering
of his gifts takes nothing away from us, we can easily
welcome the Divine being fulfilled through all. If a
particular person's genius is left untapped, we all miss
out on a fuller manifestation of God. So we actually
seek to encourage all people to be all that they are.

When we are fully engaged, we don't need to project
our own frustration and sense of unfulfillment onto

others. We are happy and want others to experience what we are experiencing, or at least the feeling of bliss that it brings. Just as misery may love company, so too does bliss!

Giving Only the Best

When we recognize that the gift we give is divine, that we are conduits for God, then we'll want to give fully, particularly when we know that our true nature is divine.

To give only the best is not about human perfection, or struggling and straining. That takes us back into unworthiness. To give the best is to make ourselves fully available to the Divine. It means that each day, each moment, we open our hearts, our minds, and our entire being as fully as we are able, to allow an avenue for that which the Divine wishes to be through us.

This is our only responsibility—to be a vessel, an instrument, a conduit through which God may use us for the benefit of all. How others accept or value what comes forth is none of our business, as long as we are not using this truth as an excuse to harm others. Our business is to give it form. As humans we cannot even know the full impact of what we do in this way. What we can know is that we have created one more outlet for heaven to be revealed on earth, and only good can come from that. It doesn't matter whether or not we can see who specifically benefits or how the whole benefits. Our satisfaction can come from just knowing that it is beneficial.

My litmus test for my actions as a child was, "What if everyone did this?" If everyone opened themselves fully to be an avenue for the goodness and grace of the Divine, the world would certainly experience a renaissance of consciousness, abundance unforeseen, and peace beyond anything experienced in the history of humankind.

To know that we are divine is to know that we are worthy of all of our gifts, talents, achievements, and any rewards that result from sharing them, including financial wealth, praise, and positive attention.

Spiritual Practices for Chapter 6

Affirmative Prayer:
There is only one: one divine essence, presence, and power. That one is Spirit, and its essence is worthiness. I am one with the One. My nature and essence is worthiness. I recognize right now that I am worthy of all the good that life has to offer. I accept the best in every area of my life. I accept the same for all others. I accept the best, I expect the best, and I give only the best of myself. I am grateful for the awareness of my worthiness. I give thanks for all the good that is right now being expressed in my life as the gift of an all-giving universe. I let this be. All is well. And so it is. Amen.

Daily Spiritual Practice:
1. Journal about how worthy you feel to receive all that makes your life fulfilling.

2. List five ideas or hidden beliefs that you are willing to let go of in order to feel more worthy.

3. List five ways that you may give more to life.

4. List ten things you are ready to have or experience in your life right now.

5. Enter meditation for at least fifteen minutes and contemplate your life as the beloved of the all-loving presence of Spirit, worthy of all the good you can imagine.

Chapter 7:
Power: Getting Our Needs Met

Recognizing Your Power

Within each one of us lies the full power of the entire universe. It is not really our power, but One Power. There is a power that responds to our attention and our intention. We create our own world of experience. This is not to say that we control everything in our experience, but we are more powerful than most of us ever imagined. There is a place within us where we connect with the infinite, the same power and force that created our physical universe.

What this means is extraordinarily important to each one of us. It means we, along with the Divine, create our experience. All wars are fought because one side feels the other side will somehow block its ability to have its needs met. In truth, we are interdependent and independent of one another. Together we can bring about so much more good in the world, and yet at the same time our good is independent of the action of any other person or nation.

Take the situation that has often been called the "oil crisis." While it might appear that some governments in the oil-producing nations have something that is vital to our existence, and therefore have power over us, really we have the power to create something different. What if we diverted our attention invested in this so-called crisis, and instead invested it in alternative energy? With that kind of investment we would have multiple sources of alternative energy and would be well on our way toward energy sufficiency.

Using Your Power for Good

Some years ago I was in a workshop for members of spiritual communities about how to use power for good. It was interesting that so many of us had a negative reaction to the word power. We associated it with evil or manipulation, or something wanted for ego purposes.

The truth is, we are powerful beyond measure, not personally, but because of our oneness with the source of all power. Power is simply the exertion of energy, will, or intent in a particular direction. It is neither good nor evil, negative nor positive. How we use it can certainly vary in terms of whether it is used constructively or destructively, but power itself is neutral.

When we are consciously on a spiritual path, it is natural to recognize our power and then use it for the benefit of all beings. We become the eyes, hands, and instruments of the infinite. We realize that while we may not be able to save the world, we can serve our fellow beings greatly. We can help to end suffering for those around us. We can be instruments for connecting others to their innate freedom. We can be conduits for helping all to get in touch with and assert their unique gifts and talents. We can be mirrors for others to see their own wholeness. We can love others so much that they begin to love themselves. In this way we reduce violence in our world as love heals all.

We can simply be present with our awake and loving consciousness to lift everything and everyone up in love and light.

Many of us don't realize that we make a difference, yet this is the truth, and especially so when we consciously allow love and light to come forth from our being. People feel our presence. Either they feel our heaviness, possibly being dragged down by it, or they feel our light and love, and are uplifted by it.

We can use our power by catching a vision of something great from the infinite and then be the vehicle through which that vision is made manifest. Perhaps it's a tutoring program for underserved youth; perhaps it's an innovation that allows more people access to food, or healthcare; perhaps it's a program for the elderly to have more companionship and attention. Whatever vision we have that energizes us and moves us, we devote ourselves to it completely. Each of us has a calling. Not every calling will put us in the public spotlight, but it will put us in alignment with the infinite and how it is seeking manifestation as us.

It is in this way that we are powerful and important. It is not personal power or importance, but our connection to the infinite.

Accepting Others' Power

Because we all have access to power, it is important that we accept and welcome others' power. We all have a right to get our needs met. When other people seem to be using their power against you, consider that they misunderstand power and have not yet understood how to use power harmoniously.

So many people fear that they won't get their needs met. Many have not yet found that infinite power exists; some commit crimes. No one who understands that he is infinitely capable of getting his needs met would steal.

In the same way, anyone who truly understands his

own access to infinite power does not fear others
exercising their power. We know that no one can take
what's ours, not because we will overpower them,
but because the power we use has no opposite. Its
use transcends conditions, circumstances, and others'
misuse of it. Certainly, people can do things that
disrupt our plans, but ultimately they cannot inhibit
our destiny—that which is ours to be, do, and have.

Using Power Collectively

There is something beautiful about working with
others to bring about good. There's a kind of magical
synergy that takes place where the whole is greater
than the sum of its parts. Somehow, together we
magnify the power of creativity and manifestation
through joining together in a common cause or
vision.

We are not islands unto ourselves. Yes, we have our
own individual destinies, but they are all intertwined
with our great collective destiny.

Together we shall rise or fall, and ultimately we shall
surely rise. It is simply our destiny.

Spiritual Practices for Chapter 7

Affirmative Prayer:
There is only one: one divine essence, presence, and
power. That one is Spirit, and its essence is power.
I am one with the One. My nature and essence is

power. Right now I accept myself as a powerful instrument of Spirit. I have the power to get my needs met. I release any judgments about my power and I see power as the gift of fulfillment. I also accept the power that works through others. All of my needs are met, and I accept the same for all others. I am grateful for the power at my center. I give thanks that my needs are continuously met. I let this be. All is well. And so it is. Amen.

Daily Spiritual Practice:

1. Journal about your thoughts and feelings about power.

2. List five ways you can step more fully into your power.

3. List five ways you could use your power toward greater good for yourself and others.

4. List five ways you could more fully accept others' power.

5. Enter meditation for at least fifteen minutes and contemplate your life as a powerful instrument of the Divine, fully capable of creating the life you choose.

Chapter 8:
Joy: Elixir of the Soul

The Joy Within

Paramahansa Yogananda wrote in his poem, "Samadhi," found in his book, *Autobiography of a Yogi,* "From joy I came, for joy I live, in sacred joy I melt." When we are in touch with the very source and essence of life itself and recognize the fullness of our own life, how could we experience anything but joy? Joy is independent of what is going on around us. Joy is an inner quality. I have often related that I have never had a bad year. Even though I have experienced the death of loved ones, career challenges, ups and downs with relationships, and all manner of human experiences, ultimately at the end of each year I have been able to honestly say, "It was good." Through it all, our souls always advance on their path. We have learned, grown, and understand better who we are and our relationship to the whole.

When we are truly conscious, there is no other possibility. Joy is an indescribable feeling and experience of wholeness and wellness, made manifest as some combination of pleasure, bliss, delight, or elation. It is life bursting forth from within to proclaim, "I am, and all is well." It is the presence of God revealed, manifested, and brought into the vibration of the individual. It is a tangible energy that is healing and soothing, with the power to transform all in its path.

I have always had fairly ready access to this vibration. At my graduation ceremony from ministerial school, we were each asked to represent a quality of the Divine. One by one, each graduate would step forth to speak a sentence or two about the given quality. When it was my turn, I stepped forward and announced my quality was joy. Before I could utter a word, the fullness of joy burst forth from my being. The whole audience got it and erupted in spontaneous applause. I never spoke a word. Everyone got it; nothing needed to be said.

That is the essence of joy—it is felt, known, and experienced. I have often walked down the street, fully in the vibration of joy, and complete strangers smile and say hello, as if to say, "Yes, I get it." The

Christian scripture in John, 12:32, says, "And I, if I be lifted up from the earth, will draw all men unto me."

This is probably true of any quality of the Divine like peace, love, and harmony. Yet joy seems to be the manifestation and embodiment of all those in their most tangible and experiential form.

Summoning Your Smile

I read something in Vietnamese Buddhist, Thich Nhat Hanh's book, *Peace Is Every Step*, that captures very well a phenomenon I have often experienced. He says, "The source of a true smile is an awakened mind." In any situation where we can bring a smile to our face, we demonstrate that we are conscious and have choice. In almost any situation, the facial muscles for smiling still function, and it is our choice how we look at it. Our smile can be a great way to consciously choose to view each situation as perfect—a way to say, "All is well."

This doesn't mean we ought to go around with a fake smile on our face all day. It means that at any moment, regardless of circumstances, we are capable of summoning a genuine smile. When we do, we touch that chord of wholeness and harmony within us, thus bringing that all-is-well vibration to our current situation.

Being a Joyful Presence

When we discover that innate joy within our being, we are capable of being a joyful presence in our world, and therefore a beneficial presence wherever we are. The conscious smile is simply a spiritual practice, and not the joy itself.

Discovering this joy comes about through conscious communion with the Divine, and through grace. Grace is always spontaneous and can never be forced, and yet it can be welcomed through our conscious communion with the presence of God within. Our openness, willingness, and receptivity to our divine nature are the opening for grace.

Because joy is our true nature, we don't have to do anything to get it. Rather than getting something, we are uncovering and revealing what is. Through grace we have shining moments of revelation and clarity, and we might say, "Aha, I've got it," but there's nothing to get, so our best course of action is to have gratitude. Give thanks for this moment of experiencing our true nature. Give thanks that now I don't just believe this is my nature, I know it. When we can't re-create the experience, we still know it is there, like the sun on a cloudy day—still there, but hidden for the moment.

Living in the state that some have called "practicing the presence" is our greatest possibility for being a benefit to the planet. In doing so, we are raising the vibration of the whole planet. We become an opening, a vehicle, and a vessel through which more of heaven can be revealed on earth. Not heaven as a place, but heaven as a vibration of wholeness, harmony, and love.

Being conscious means we get to choose heaven or hell, moment by moment. Being unconscious, heaven and hell are imposed on our experience by the ever-changing circumstances and conditions of our lives.

Joy is something we can choose moment by moment. Joy is always available within us, regardless of what is happening in our outer experience. My invitation is to cultivate that joy within you. At first, you may need to do it while outer circumstances make it easy to be joyful. When that happens, pay close attention to what it feels like and to what the state of being is for you. Then, even when you don't have outer confirmation, you'll have inner remembrance of a state of being that you can choose, and joy will always be yours.

Spiritual Practices for Chapter 8

Affirmative Prayer:
There is only one: one divine essence, presence, and power. That one is Spirit, and its essence is joy. I am one with the One. My nature and essence is joy. I open myself to experience joy. Joy is my nature. It is a joy that transcends circumstances and conditions. I allow joy to have free sway in my life. Joy flows through me in infinite measure from my center. For this I am grateful. I give thanks for this continuous availability of joy. I let this be. All is well. And so it is. Amen.

Daily Spiritual Practice:
1. Journal about your experience of joy. Where do you feel it in your body? Where does it originate?
2. List five ways you could cultivate more joy in your life.
3. List five things you could release from your life to experience more joy.
4. List five ways you could be a more joyful presence in the world.
5. Enter meditation for at least fifteen minutes and contemplate your life with the continuous availability of eternal joy at your center.

Chapter 9:
Freedom: The Spirit Demands It

Attaining Personal Freedom

How much freedom do you have? What are you free
to do or be? In principle, you have infinite freedom,
the power to be or do anything that allows your soul
to fulfill its highest calling. But is this your experience?
Do you feel you have infinite freedom? If not, what
limits you?

What limits most of us is how we think about life.
I talked to a man once who said he felt it was more
difficult for him to change his career now while in
his forties than it would have been in his thirties. I
suggested to him that the only real difference is in

how he thought about himself in his thirties and how he thinks of himself now. He lit up when I mentioned this idea. It resonated with him.

We can have as much freedom as we can conceive, certainly on the level of being, and usually on the level of doing and having. Our power to create and to manifest is unlimited. We must first dare to conceive of a greater idea, a greater vision for our lives. A small, narrow, and limited vision of one's self, and of life, will never create a sense of great freedom. Only a grand vision combined with the awareness that manifestation follows vision, with certainty, will create a sense of great freedom. Philosopher Ernest Holmes said, "Principle is not bound by precedent." In other words, the causative creative forces of life are not in the least influenced by the past. They are influenced only by the state of our consciousness now.

If we can expand our consciousness now, with a greater vision, more acceptance of the goodness available to us, and greater faith in the creative power within us, then we can create the life of our dreams, irrespective of the past. We can begin now to create a life of great freedom. Of course, it will look different for each of us. What does a life of great freedom look like to you? What would your life be like if you were totally free?

Removing Our Binds on Others
One of the first steps toward gaining a greater sense of freedom for ourselves is to release others spiritually

and metaphorically. We can't hold others in bondage and simultaneously be free ourselves. What we want for ourselves, we must give to others, and we must want it for others and celebrate it in them. Celebrate anytime you see someone experiencing the type of freedom you wish to experience, whether friend or foe. Celebrate it as a demonstration to you that it's possible for you. If it is possible for someone else, then it is possible for you. Let go of the idea that "things like that only happen to other people." Recognize the other person as a mirror, and that you are simply seeing what is beginning to manifest for you.

Every time you see evidence of this type of freedom showing up in your life, celebrate that, too. Give thanks—"Yes, my vision is being made real." Every time you do that, you create more fertile ground for your vision to be made manifest.

Confronting Fear
Marianne Williamson, in her book, *A Return to Love*, said, "Our deepest fear is not that we are inadequate. Our deepest fear is that we are powerful beyond measure." Our greatest fear is usually not that we cannot attain our vision, but that we will. For many of us, our greatest dream or vision is too big and too good to even think or imagine. Some ask themselves, "Could I even step into such a large vision? Am I worthy of it?" Even though we catch a grand vision, we often dismiss it, either consciously or unconsciously, as merely a pipe dream, or something possible for someone, but surely not for us.

To attain great freedom, we must address fear. First, we must realize that fear is an experience we have. It is not who we are. Although it may feel overwhelming at times, it doesn't mean it truly has power over us. In fact, when we realize that fear is just an experience rooted in the world and has nothing to do with who we are in our essence, then we can begin to be free from the effects of fear. We don't really need to be free of the experience of fear, so long as we realize it is just a human experience. Once we put it in that context, it no longer rules us. We can become the observer of this experience. As the observer, we have the freedom to decide what we will do with the experience, or how we will respond to it.

Consider this metaphor: A being called Fear knocks at the door of a one-room house. I answer the door rather than resist Fear. I welcome Fear to come in the house. I walk it across the room, all the while speaking lovingly to it—"Welcome back, Fear. What brings you this way again? You know I have nothing against you, but I don't base my life on you anymore. So you are welcome to visit, but not welcome to stay." Then I gently and lovingly guide Fear across the room and out the door on the other side. This is a metaphor for how we may experience the sensation of fear in our bodies. It rises from somewhere, perhaps the pit of our stomach, and rather than pushing it down, we allow it to rise and then pass through us. Without our resistance, fear becomes a momentary experience, not something we live with constantly.

In allowing fear to pass through us, we also have the great opportunity to understand fear, and what it specifically represents for us. What triggers your fear? And what about that triggers your fear? And what is under that? Peel back the layers of the onion. Explore, be aware, observe, welcome the experience, embrace it, and allow it to teach you about what gets in your way. Now, do you see the gift in it?

Does your fear come up when others have a lot of freedom? What's that about? Again, peel back the layers. Journaling is good for this purpose. As you observe the experience of fear, write about it in a journal. Describe it. Don't get caught up in the details or the story. Allow the process to open the way to greater clarity and understanding.

Living from Love

Living from love is the opposite of living from fear. Living from love allows one to ask, "How can I serve? How can I benefit others? How may I most fully be engaged in life? There's no attempt to do it right, or to get the approval of others. There is simply the pure intent to give all that we have to life, to others, and to ourselves. This is true freedom. When we simply give the best and let go of all the rest, allowing this moment to be sufficient, we are free.

Nothing is missing and nothing can be added. All has been given, and that is enough. We can sleep well and in peace. I gave all I had today. Tomorrow is a new day. We release concern over how the gifts we give are received. Ours is only to give all with love. There's no judgment, criticism, doubt, or fear. My intent is to love, and that is enough.

If we give all we have of our gifts, talents, energies, and substance from a place of love, with the only intent as love, we are freed from the rest. We are freed from self-doubt—"What if others don't like my gift?" We are freed from fear—"What if I don't do it right?" We are freed from judgment—"What if I didn't do enough?"

This simple practice of living from love, from a pure intention of love, is a key ingredient to achieving the freedom we want.

Spiritual Practices for Chapter 9

Affirmative Prayer:
There is only one: one divine essence, presence, and power. That one is Spirit, and its essence is freedom. I am one with the One. My nature and essence is freedom. I release every idea of bondage, lack, or limitation. I am free to experience the life of my soul's highest calling. I am totally free: free to be me, free to choose my experiences, free to be fully expressed, free to be happy, free to be prosperous, and free to experience the fullness of life. I am grateful for my freedom. I give thanks for all the fruits of my freedom. I let this be. All is well. And so it is. Amen.

Daily Spiritual Practice:

1. Journal about what a life of total freedom would look like for you.

2. List five ideas or hidden beliefs you are willing to let go of so you can experience more freedom.

3. List five ideas or ways of being that you are willing to embrace to experience more freedom.

4. Choose three steps you will take this week that represent your greater freedom.

5. Enter meditation for at least fifteen minutes and contemplate your life as one having absolute freedom.

Chapter 10:
Surrender: It's Bigger Than You

Examining the Need to Control

While we certainly have dominion in our lives and can direct our lives to some degree, how much control do we really have? If we just look at the human body we see so many things that take place without our control, or even our awareness—cells regenerating, lungs breathing, heart beating, food digesting, and seemingly an infinite array of activities taking place, none of which we are consciously directing. The very creation of the body we are in, including skin color, gender, height, and body type, was all established without our conscious awareness.

Surely, at a soul level we may have chosen much of that, or at least it was the natural result of our soul's path, but we could hardly call it control. Even our achievements in life, which we may feel we controlled or directed, still had elements of luck, grace, or whatever we want to call it. Sure, we put in a lot of hard work and overcame many obstacles, but if we examine our accomplishments closely, we shall have to admit that there were so many things that just fell into place.

Of course, we did put ourselves into that flow to be in a position for them to fall into place, so it is not to say that we had no role. It is simply that we didn't have full control. Many who exerted the same effort that we did were not triumphant, or at least not in the same way. Of course, there were times when we have fallen short, at least momentarily, even when we have given our all.

What we ultimately gain some control over is ourselves. We govern our choices, our attention, our intention, and the exertion of our energy in particular directions. From that we set things in motion that correspond to the direction of our intentions. Yet, we are not actually controlling all that takes place.

Although largely an illusion, it is quite human to desire control. Our ego's tendency is to want to be in control. Because of this illusion, humans are greatly afraid of losing that control. It seems that our very physical survival is at risk, and perhaps this stems from the human survival instinct.

We had better control our body when crossing
the street, lest we stray into traffic. We had better
control ourselves in the presence of fire, lest we burn
ourselves. These are natural uses of control that
support our functioning in this world, in this body.

However, when we overly extend that into trying
to control people, circumstances, and events, then
we begin to limit ourselves, and often cause more
difficulty for ourselves than we need to.

Letting Go, Letting Go, Letting Go

The human urge is to try to control, and yet the
soul functions best when it is allowed to flow forth
unimpeded. There is such wisdom at the soul level.
Letting go is letting our soul have its full sway with
us. It is aligning with the higher nature and purpose
of our being. The truly great achievements in art,
music, and invention come forth through an act of
surrender.

The human mind is great at building on what came
before and using previously known concepts, but
greatness demands more. It requires reaching into that
transcendent realm of unconditioned being, opening
ourselves to see what previously has not been seen.

When we let go, we do as Ralph Waldo Emerson
admonished us to do—get our "bloated nothingness
out of the way." In letting go, we are not going on
blind faith. We are actually relying on that infinite
wisdom and power of the soul to create. As we

commune with the divine presence that is our soul's connection to the whole, we are actually cooperating with our infinite nature rather than our finite. We are expressing from that infinite nature, so our outcomes and our creative expression reflect the transcendent qualities of the soul. We are then prepared to reveal heaven on earth. Heaven is not a place, but an infinite realm of possibility that we can experience now, to the degree that we open to it.

Being an Instrument of the Divine

Being an instrument of the Divine, a surrendered vessel, means being willing to continuously choose the path that honors the highest calling of the soul, no matter whether this path is uncomfortable or blissful. With that choice come clarity, freedom, and strength.

In being an instrument through which the Divine can work, there is nothing to control. We are allowing something to happen that is bigger than us in a human sense and yet is us of our highest essence.

Our only question becomes, how would my soul like to be expressed? In other words, what is my highest expression in this moment? If we are making a decision, we simply ask, which choice will allow the greatest unfolding of my soul?

Strength and clarity come from getting ourselves out of the way. It is no longer my will, but "thy will be done." The first metaphysical author I read, Jiddu Krishnamurti, is quoted as saying toward the end of his teaching days that his secret was, "I don't mind what happens." This is the attitude we can take when we surrender to the highest calling of our soul. It is not that we don't care anymore. It is simply that we have stepped into such a degree of willingness to serve a higher calling, that our human needs just seem secondary. Probably most of us would agree that the unfolding of our soul is more important than this or that job, this or that partner. Ultimately, the highest calling of our soul is, in fact, that which brings us the greatest satisfaction as humans. However, it just may require us to step out of our comfort zone first.

The Surrendered Life

Living the surrendered life is making choices from the place of our soul's highest calling. What choices align us with the greatest unfolding and expression of our soul? How do we know this? How do we live this way? The short answer is spiritual practice—more specifically, daily meditation. Meditation is the practice that allows us to commune with the Divine, to listen deeply to the call of our soul.

There are so many voices within to distinguish— those of our parents, society, authority figures, the voice of comfort, the voice of safety and security, the voice of vanity. Even with all of these voices active at various times, the voice of our soul is distinct, and we can learn to recognize it and listen to it.

The distinction is more qualitative than logical or rational. The soul's voice is felt, sensed, and perceived rather than thought. It is generally gentler, softer, less insistent, more matter of fact, and less attached than the other voices. It speaks and waits for us to listen. Of course, eventually it can seem very loud simply because we can no longer ignore it.

At some point, when our soul is calling us to do or become something, our whole being resonates so much with that calling that the soul's voice is amplified. This amplifiation doesn't change the nature of the soul's voice any more than a microphone changes the voice of a singer. It simply makes that still small voice loud for that moment.

By communing with the presence of Spirit, we engage in the divine courtship. We begin to court a closer relationship with our higher nature. It is a courtship with a very willing participant. However, because our divinity is usually noninsistent, it awaits our acceptance, our welcome, and our overtures.

Many writers and mystics, including philosopher Ernest Holmes, have spoken of the human giving way to the Divine, or about the shortfalls of being double-minded. When we begin to place our entire attention and intention on the cultivation of our soul and welcoming it into expression, then the soul's voice becomes readily available to us. All of the promises of metaphysics, modern spirituality, and ancient wisdom become more real for us in our day-to-day experience.

The promises of divine wisdom, creativity, intelligence, and prosperity all become more real to us simply because we are living closer to the source and in alignment with the nature of our divinity.

It is our truest nature to experience the promises, but this is difficult when we are not living in alignment with our truest nature. Living in alignment is consciously choosing to acknowledge our true nature, and allowing other aspects of our being to have their proper place. The Christian scripture in Luke 20:25 says, "Render therefore unto Caesar the things which be Caesar's, and unto God the things which be God's."

Things of the world are here for us to enjoy and appreciate. They throw us off only when we treat them as if they were the source of our fulfillment, rather than the fruits from the source that they truly are.

Living the surrendered life is continuously living in the awareness of our true nature and the awareness that God is the source of all that is. It is listening for our soul's path and following it. It is taking care of our human needs while having our greatest attention on the needs of our soul. In truth, both needs are directly connected.

Living in surrender means giving up the illusion of control. Since we aren't really in control of very much anyway, we really aren't giving up very much, yet through the conscious act of surrender, we are gaining so much. I encourage you to let go just a little in this moment, and then a little more and a little more. Let the human give way to the Divine, so that your higher nature is tapped and you reap all the promises of the spiritual teachings of the ages. You deserve to be fulfilled. Surrender is the way.

Spiritual Practices for Chapter 10

Affirmative Prayer:
There is only one: one divine essence, presence, and power. That one is Spirit, and its essence is surrender. I am one with the One. My nature and essence is surrender. I now let go of the illusion of control. All of life is working for me, and nothing is working against me; therefore I find nothing to resist or control. I now surrender and allow Spirit to move through me, as me. Through my surrender to Spirit I accomplish great works. For this surrender I am so grateful. I give thanks for all of the good that surrender brings into my life. I let this be. All is well. And so it is. Amen.

Daily Spiritual Practice:
1. Journal about what a surrendered life looks like to you.
2.List five ways you feel the need to control events, circumstances, or people. Are you willing to let these go?
3. Remember a time when you fully surrendered and describe what that felt like.

4. List three steps you are willing to take this week toward a surrendered life.

5. Enter meditation for at least fifteen minutes and contemplate your life completely surrendered to Spirit.

Chapter 11:
Caring: You Have Done
It unto Me

Jesus is quoted as saying in the Christian scripture,
Matthew 25:40, "Inasmuch as ye have done it unto
one of the least of these my brethren, ye have done
it unto me." In truth, whatever we do to another,
we do to ourselves and to all others. Our actions are
like ripples upon a lake. They fan out to touch the
multitudes and cannot be limited to just the people
we intend. That goes for love and caring, just as much
as it does for harmful acts. Our actions go forth to
either bless or diminish all life.

Honoring All Life

One of the greatest ways we can honor life is to honor
and cherish our planet. This beautiful, alive planet upon
which we live deserves to be free of toxins, pollution,
insecticides, and commercial waste products. Because
collectively we have not had this as a value, we have
done much damage. A good example is with pesticides.
Clearly the success of organic products shows us we
can farm without pesticides. Unfortunately, we humans,
in so many areas of life, often prefer the quick and easy
route, regardless of the harmful effects. Insects are a
valuable part of our ecosystem. The idea of pesticides
presumes that only we human beings are entitled to the
bounty of life produced by our planet. This ignores
the nature of the food chain and the delicate balance
nature has created for us. The natural state of the
planet is a lush cornucopia. Just visit any areas of forest
that are untouched by humans and this is evident. We
must be mindful not to let greed and shortsighted
thinking compromise or interfere with this beautiful,
divine harmony that is ready to provide for all.

When we honor all life, we honor God. God is life
expressed in all its forms. I remember being at a
ten-day Buddhist silent meditation retreat where one
of the rules was that we could not kill during our time
there. This seemed like an unnecessary rule for those
on a spiritual path with enough dedication to spend
ten days in silence, until I got to my room and found
a mosquito. My first inclination was to immediately
extinguish its life. Then, quickly I remembered what
I had agreed to. Could I break the rules on the first

day of this ten-day journey? I didn't, and I don't recall even getting bitten.

When we realize that all creatures are God's creation, each serving a unique and important purpose, we can begin to honor and even feel a sense of reverence toward them all.

Because all of life is truly one, we diminish in some way all of life whenever we diminish any life. Whatever you have done to the least of these my brethren, you have done it unto me.

Letting Go of Judgment

Judgment is one the most self-destructive acts we can engage in. There's the saying that when we point our finger at someone, three fingers are pointing back at us. This is true in more than just an anatomical sense. Judgment has to pass through our own consciousness first before it ever goes forth to touch another. Therefore, it creates in our own experience something that resembles the very thing we are condemning. In some way, in some form, it will show up in the life of the one judging.

Aside from its causative effects in our own life, judgment is a violent act toward the one whom we are judging and a violent act toward ourselves. When we judge others, we are seeing imperfection, seeing them as less than whole. We are finding something unacceptable in them personally. This is the difference between condemning an act (i.e., something harmful that was done) and condemning the person who did it. If we really understand truth, we know that "there, but for the grace of God go I" as a sixteenth-century English reformer, John Bradford said.

It is important to consider, how am I in relationship with life? Some things align us with our highest nature and put us in the flow of life, and others move us away into a sense of separation. Judgment moves us into separation. Separation is a state of disconnecting from the source. We are not truly separate, but our judgment can put us in a position where we experience what looks and feels like separation.

When we truly understand the interconnectedness of all life and that we cannot condemn another without condemning ourselves, then we naturally let go of judgments.

Otherwise we can end up being a point in consciousness that is dislodged and blocks the flow within the interconnected life. Instead, we could be an opening for the flow of love and light.

Harmful acts have their own consequences. We don't have to impose that. Harmful acts put those people committing them in a converse relationship with life, thereby creating any number of detrimental effects upon themselves. This is not God condemning them. It is their own actions and intentions condemning them. Such people need our compassion rather than our judgment.

Cultivating Empathy and Compassion

Empathy and compassion will not only move us out of judgment, but will also take us a long way toward forgiveness. When we have resentment and anger toward another, we often feel that the person shouldn't have done what he did and that something evil in him caused him to do it. However, when we really work toward empathy and compassion, we begin to see that the actions are more about the person's relationship with himself, with life, and with his own divine nature, and the result can be harmful to others. We don't have to condone his behavior or even remove consequences. Our intention of empathy and compassion shifts our energetic relationship to the person and the situation. We are no longer angry and resentful toward the person or situation. Love is now what connects us.

Really, there is no reason to be angry with anyone. Brief feelings of anger notwithstanding, we need not hold onto anger and resentment. We need not experience life through that vibration. It is not helpful to us or to anyone else.

Cultivating empathy and compassion is about connecting to love, connecting to the source, God. Love is our nature. Love heals all. "Forgive them; for they know not what they do," Jesus is purported to have said on the cross in some versions of Christian scripture (Luke 23:34). Some would say, "Sure, they knew what they were doing." In a sense this might be true, but in the sense of consciousness, no one who is fully conscious of the presence of God as his very life and the life of all others, could act in any way other than the way of love. When we awaken to the truth of our divinity and the divinity of all others, we are capable of only love.

Your awakening to this truth frees you to embrace every being in love, no matter what he may have done to you, or attempted to do to you. You no longer blame people for their consciousness. They are wherever they are, given their present level of awareness. In that regard, they are truly doing the best they can.

When we condemn and judge, we are operating out of the same consciousness as the one who performed the harmful act, and then no one wins. "An eye for an eye leaves the whole world blind," is a quote often attributed to Mohandas Gandhi. Instead of "an eye for an eye" unconsciousness, let us be conscious. When we're conscious, it is simple to feel empathy, compassion, and love for every being. After all, there are individuals who are more conscious than you and I. Do we deserve their condemnation? Of course not. We are all on this path together, experiencing it at whatever degree of awareness we have. It's not wrong to be at any place along the path, nor is there a right place to be. We just are where we are, and that is perfect.

Let us embrace all beings everywhere. Let our response to everyone be from love.

Sacred Service to Life

When we cultivate our awareness of the Divine as our
very life and the life of all beings, we are in a great
position to serve humanity and all life. We are no
longer part of the problem, but instead we are part of
awakening all to their spiritual magnificence. We are
now part of raising the vibration in our world. We are
no longer so much in the debate, the struggle, or the
mentality of survival of the fittest. We are no longer
moved by the various wars and rumors of wars. We
no longer have any enemies, opponents, or anyone to
fear. All beings are our beloveds and the beloveds of
the most high. We can be trusted because all feel our
neutrality and impartiality. All feel our love. We are
for all and against none. We are not for all actions, but
we are for all beings. We affirm their wholeness and
perfection. We neither condemn nor accept harmful
actions. We recognize the consciousness from which
they came, and we work on raising the vibration.

A higher vibration, a greater alignment with our
divinity, always leads to a greater result. This is our
only work—using our consciousness to lift the
vibration in our world.

We don't have to fix anything, or decide which side
of an issue we're on, or fight for or oppose anything.
These are all in the world of effects. Anything done in
that consciousness will simply create more effects like
itself. Acting from the perspective of separation and
division creates more separation and division.

Acting from the perspective of wholeness, oneness, and win-win raises us above polarities and lose-lose scenarios, and into a place where we all win.

Yes, we all can win. No one has to lose, but everyone has to change. We all have to let go of our rigid thinking about how we get our needs met, so that the larger vision of a world that works for everyone can be revealed and manifested.

While we hold so tightly to petty things, life is trying to offer us much more. First we have to let go of our limited sense of what's possible. Then we open to the greater possibility that wants to unfold in our life, for all life.

Spiritual Practices for Chapter 11

Affirmative Prayer:
There is only one: one divine essence, presence, and power. That one is Spirit, and its essence is caring. I am one with the One. My nature and essence is caring. Today I allow myself to care deeply about other beings. I open my heart so that all beings everywhere may be happy and well. I care about and for myself, and for every being. I have a heart of love and compassion. My heart is open to give and receive love. I give thanks for my nature of love, compassion, and caring. I am grateful for the loving world I am experiencing and helping to create. I let this be. All is well. And so it is. Amen.

Daily Spiritual Practice:
1. Journal about what being caring and compassionate means to you.
2. List five ways you could honor all of life more.
3. List five ways you could care for and honor yourself more.
4. List five judgments you could release about others in order to be more caring and compassionate.
5. Enter meditation for at least fifteen minutes and contemplate your life as one who is deeply cared for by all of life, and as one who deeply cares for others.

Chapter 12:
Oneness: The Antidote
to Separation

Seeing God in Everything
We live in a world with many dualistic messages. We are taught to compete at a very young age. We are taught directly and indirectly about scarcity and lack. We learn lose-lose models. We sometimes treat our bodies as machines, disconnected from life itself.

Spiritual teachers and mystics have taught about oneness and wholeness for ages. Now quantum physics and science are beginning to prove oneness and how connected all things are.

What does it mean to see God in everything? One way to look at it is to see life in everything. Everything is alive with the same essence. There is an is-ness to everything. There is an inherent neutrality in everything and yet a leaning in the direction of growth, expansion, and even love.

To see God in everything is to see each person's inherent neutrality and then to call forth the highest vibration from it. People and situations are rarely good or bad in and of themselves. Rather, all is waiting for us to call it good and lift it into a higher vibration.

Because life, or God, is present right where you are and has no real boundaries, your presence of life is connected to and one with everything in your environment. All life is connected to all other life, and everything in between is connected in that same web. It is all one field, seemingly separated by illusory boundaries, yet in reality, one.

How often have you thought of someone and then he or she called or showed up? How often have you envisioned something, and then had it manifest in your life? How could this be possible in a world where everything is separate? Some might call this a coincidence, and yet if you begin to cultivate your awareness of this reality, you will see that it happens much more often than coincidence could explain. Everything is connected to everything else. All of life is connected.

Your recognition of that simply activates it more fully in your life. Our opportunity is to live each moment in this awareness. Then we become conduits of oneness, and pure instruments for connection.

When we see God in everything, we magnify our connection to everything. In doing so, we open ourselves more to the flow of divine goodness and the giving nature of the Divine. We align with a higher truth and we move ourselves into that realm where only good can come to us, and harm cannot come near us.

When we look for God in everything, we find it. This means looking for the good, or the gift, in all people and in all situations. It is there. Only people and situations that serve our spiritual path are possible in our experience.

Certainly, we have a great deal of choice about what comes into our experience, and our goal is to choose consciously. Whether we draw things and people consciously or unconsciously, they are ultimately there to serve our spiritual path. Then we can consciously choose, through our inner divine wisdom, what to do or how to be with each experience.

Knowing Only God
God is the ultimate reality. It is the intelligence, principle, and presence behind all things. Therefore, there is nothing to know but God, and the only way to know is through God. All knowing is God

knowing itself. God is the infinite knower and God is the knowing.

To know only God is to focus on the highest within us. It is to commune with the infinite presence of Spirit within our being and within all being. Ultimately, we are all one being. There is no separation. In the physical realm there are apparent boundaries, but even these are illusions as science is discovering great connectivity and correlation between all things. The great reality is that each point is a center of pure consciousness, pure light, pure being. As Spirit, it has no boundaries in time and space.

In truth, we are each infinite beings. Our bodies have finite boundaries, but our bodies are not the full extent of our being. Our bodies are mere vessels and vehicles with which to travel through this world of form. Who we are is consciousness—a center of infinite consciousness. The degree of infiniteness that we experience is relative to the degree we are conscious of it.

To know only God is to be a pure conduit of love and light. What a tremendous presence of healing and transformation we can be in our world.

One could say our only real purpose is to know who we are as divine beings and to know all others as divine. When we touch that divine reality, nothing else matters. Our only intention becomes to live in that divine reality. It is the reality described in the Christian scripture in Matthew 6:33: "Seek ye first the kingdom of God, and his righteousness; and all these things shall be added unto you."

Our meditations and other spiritual practices serve to tap us into this divine reality. Our conscious choice is to be on a spiritual path, to diligently live in the now. The experience of this divine reality is always available to us, not just while we're seated in deep meditation. It is not meant to be something we refer to as having had a "good meditation." The good meditation is an opening or glimpse into a divine reality that is ever available.

To live in communion with this divine reality moment by moment is to know only God, and is to be a greatly beneficial presence in the world.

Embodying Christ Consciousness

To embody Christ consciousness is truly our one and only goal. Here I don't mean Christ as the last name of Jesus, but rather as the consciousness that Jesus and other enlightened beings embodied and lived, including the Buddha, Mohammad, Krishna, and others. These beings who achieved an enlightened state show us what's possible for each of us. They themselves need not be worshipped. Instead, they are to be emulated.

Is it possible, we might ask, to emulate Jesus or the Buddha? The answer is yes—it is our destiny to do so.

We might do this, perhaps, in this lifetime, or perhaps not, or perhaps for this moment, or perhaps not. There is a window into the divine light that already resides right within our own being and all around us. It is not a place for us to arrive. Rather, it is about recognizing who and what we already are.

To embody Christ consciousness is to live most fully in our true nature. To live in our true nature is to live from love. It is to see, feel, sense, and know our oneness with all that is. It is to commune with that infinite wellspring of love and light at the center of our own being. It is to surrender to such a degree that there is nothing to surrender to—I and my Father/ Mother God are one. It is to be a willing vessel, fully available to the divine urge to express through us. It is to let go of fear and doubt for good.

How do we do this? There is nothing to do as much as there is something to become. There is nothing to become as much as there is the letting go of all that binds us and blinds us. We must find the willingness to take time each day to stop doing, and in the stillness, be willing to discover the higher truth of our being. We get to let go of our identity with all the random thoughts and chatter that enter our minds. Let them enter, since we cannot stop them anyway. Let them be. Don't claim them to be yours, anymore than you would claim the chatter on the radio to be yours. Let it be and turn away from it. Turn toward your desire to know God, to know your true nature.

Remember that what you are discovering is the truth of who you already are. It is so simple that it is easy to miss. We have to stop trying so hard. Just be open, patient, willing, committed, and persistent. To know your true nature is the greatest gift, so give it all of your attention. This does not mean just during your meditation. We also need to mindfully give attention during our daily tasks, routines, work, and interactions. Awaken. Don't just go through your day acting from habitual patterns in a rote manner. Instead, choose to be conscious. Be the observer of your life and particularly of your feelings, reactions, and how you respond to what is happening. What triggers you, either positively or negatively? Don't judge—just observe. This is how you mindfully give attention. This is how you awaken. This is how you become conscious. This is how you discover your true nature. Moment by moment, you are awake and aware.

As you live from this place, you begin to see more and more. You get to see what you identify with, where your attachments are, what triggers fear in you, and all of the other elements that keep you from seeing and experiencing your true nature.

Peel back the "layers of the onion." Watch your inner dialogue and engage with it. Your dialogue might go like this: "Hmm, isn't that interesting that I'm feeling fear right now?" Notice that you are not identifying with the fear. It is not your fear. It is simply a sensation that you are experiencing, something triggered within you. Don't try to change the fear or push it down. You simply observe it. Let it inform you. Watch and see where it comes from. Where do you feel it in your body? What is its nature? Feel it fully, and eventually watch it pass.

Many don't meditate because they are afraid of what they might find. They don't want to face what might be there out of fear that it might overwhelm them, that it has some power over them. It does not have power. In fact, when observed with our detached awareness, we see that it is merely a string of sensations—the activity of neurological synapses and habitual patterns of thinking and reacting, things not really powerful at all unto themselves.

What is powerful is our ability to choose. What we choose is what we will do with all of these patterns built into our nervous system. Do we choose to give them power or do we choose to just observe them? In observing them, we can recognize that they are not who we are, but rather they are conditioned responses based on past thinking, beliefs, attitudes, choices, and even the nature of our humanness. Can we see that we can begin to think, believe, and choose differently?

For example, if we realize that a fear has no rational basis, we can allow the sensation associated with the fear to do whatever it does, while at the same time not act from the irrational fear. Instead, we act from what we know to be true for us, despite a sensation going on in the body that we might label as fear.

When we begin to act from this quality of awareness, we begin to free ourselves from habitual patterns of thinking and reacting. Our actions are more thoughtful, more creative, and more connected to the present moment. Our choices are conscious. They are no longer the result of conditioned behavior. The internal mind chatter and reactions within our nervous system may remain the same for some time, but our actions and our conscious thinking take on a whole new quality. Eventually, the old conditioned patterns begin to lose their grip altogether.

There is an awakening to which all of humanity is being called. It is the opening to the end of war, poverty, and other conditions that affect our world. These conditions are all the result of stale patterns of thinking and acting. By awakening to our true nature, we see through the illusion that allows war to exist in spite of concrete evidence that it creates more longstanding problems than it resolves.

In awakening, new possibilities reveal themselves, new solutions that are not based in fear, but instead are based in mindfully choosing that which reflects insights into our very nature—and therefore holds promise for longstanding success and the evolution of the human species.

All of this is accomplished first by recognizing that we are not separate from anything or anyone. We are one with all life. Because of this, a change we make within ourselves has great power to transform our planet. We are utterly vital.

Spiritual Practices for Chapter 12

Affirmative Prayer:
There is only one: one divine essence, presence, and power. That one is Spirit, and its essence is oneness. I am one with the One. My nature and essence is oneness. Everywhere I look, I see Spirit. In all that I do, say, and think, I recognize Spirit right there in the midst of me. My life is the life of Spirit expressing. I now relax into knowing that all is well in my life, for it is all Spirit. I give thanks for this awareness of Spirit as the all in all, as all. I give thanks that life is for me, and for all others. I let this be. All is well. And so it is. Amen.

Daily Spiritual Practice:
1. Journal about your experience or imagination of the interconnectedness of all of life.
2. List five ways you see the Divine and sacred in everyday things.
3. List three ideas or hidden beliefs in separateness that you are willing to release.
4. List five ways you are willing to offer the fruits of your spiritual path to all of life.
5. Enter meditation for at least fifteen minutes and contemplate your life as one with all of life.

Conclusion

It is my intention that you use the insights and spiritual practices from this book to rise above the lowest common denominator of lose-lose scenarios. We are at a point of great possibility with our human civilization. We collectively know everything we need to know to create peace on earth and a place where all can thrive by expressing their gifts and talents.

Through our individual and collective spiritual practice, it is now time to become that greater place of peace, love, and harmony. And it is time to share this awareness with all whom we meet.

I hope you see that the ideas in this book are more than mere platitudes and wishful thinking. They are, in truth, a reality awaiting each one's discovery. They point to a world waiting to be created, not by a government or those whom we call our leaders, but by the people. That is, by ordinary people like you and me who begin to transform our own ways of being and how we live our lives. Particularly we must change how we relate to one another and how we view one another.

As we all begin to see clearly our interconnectedness and our common destiny, not just theoretically, but as an experienced reality, we can create the world I am describing here. This can come about only through daily spiritual practice and through a conscious approach to life whereby we are continuously expanding our awareness of what no longer serves us. As we continuously embrace a new idea, a new truth of who we are and of what this life is, we bring about change.

Thankfully, this journey we are embarking on together is not a somber life of austerity. It is a joyful opening to constant new discoveries in our inner realm that have profound impacts on our outer experience of life and our ability to support and serve others. First, we must take care of things at home, within our own being. We must leave the ranks of the walking wounded, so that we are the healed and whole. That way we can come to the situations in the world and transcend them, rather than participate at the same level of the problem in the same consciousness that created it.

Our "yes" to this journey is all that is required. There is no one more qualified than you. Perhaps there are some who are further along the path, but rest assured, they don't have anything that you don't have within you waiting to be discovered.

For sure, our expanded awareness at times can be difficult, especially when we are called to look more deeply at who we have been. Our concepts of our self will have to shift, both in terms of seeing how we are greater than we have thought, but also in terms of seeing how we have contributed to the problems in our lives and in our world.

It will require our courage and honesty to look at ourselves and continue to step into the greater and greater possibilities, and to continue to release what no longer serves. As you do step into the greater possibilities, always remember that every embrace of something new requires a release of what was. Our human tendency sometimes is to try to keep adding, not letting go of anything. Letting go is as important, if not more important, as expanding.

Know that you are up to the task. Know that you are here for this work of tending to your soul, and to the collective soul of humanity. There is a common saying that you can't take it with you. The work on your consciousness, the healing of your soul, you can take that with you.

May you reveal your soul's highest calling, live that calling, and transform the planet along the way. I extend my love and blessings to you, my fellow spiritual traveler. I am humbled and honored to walk this path with you and to know that we together are creating a world that works for everyone by revealing each one's spiritual magnificence.

About the Author

Gregory Toole is the Director of Member Support and Education for Centers for Spiritual Living in Golden, Colorado, which is dedicated to helping individuals discover the spiritual tools and inner resources to transform their personal lives and make the world a better place. There he oversees and leads the educational and spiritual development programs serving its many centers, practitioners, and spiritual leaders around the world. In addition, he expresses his gifts as a writer, speaker, and teacher, and has been referred to as a modern-day mystic.

Gregory grew up in Philadelphia, Pennsylvania, where at a very young age he was intrigued with spirituality and the deep mystical questions of life. He followed a traditional path of education, including a master's degree in management from MIT, and embarked on a very successful corporate career. After twelve years in this career, Gregory felt a strong pull to be of greater service to humanity. At the time it was not clear how this was to manifest, but it was very clear that his corporate career was complete and that he was to embark on something new. Shortly thereafter he discovered his love of working with youth and became executive director of a local youth development organization in Oakland, California. Over the next several years he completed the studies and practice to become a licensed spiritual practitioner and ordained minister with Centers for Spiritual Living. He was the spiritual leader for one of its centers in Northern California before stepping into his current role at the hub of the movement.